IN ASSOCIATION
WITH

Hodder Gibson
Model Practice
Papers
WITH ANSWERS

PLUS: Official SQA Specimen Paper
With Answers

Higher for CfE
French

2014 Specimen Question Paper
& Model Papers

HODDER
GIBSON
AN HACHETTE UK COMPANY

This book contains the official 2014 SQA Specimen Question Paper for Higher for CfE French, with associated SQA approved answers modified from the official marking instructions that accompany the paper.

In addition the book contains model practice papers, together with answers, plus study skills advice. These papers, some of which may include a limited number of previously published SQA questions, have been specially commissioned by Hodder Gibson, and have been written by experienced senior teachers and examiners in line with the new Higher for CfE syllabus and assessment outlines, Spring 2014. This is not SQA material but has been devised to provide further practice for Higher for CfE examinations in 2015 and beyond.

Hodder Gibson is grateful to the copyright holders, as credited on the final page of the Answer Section, for permission to use their material. Every effort has been made to trace the copyright holders and to obtain their permission for the use of copyright material. Hodder Gibson will be happy to receive information allowing us to rectify any error or omission in future editions.

Hachette UK's policy is to use papers that are natural, renewable and recyclable products and made from wood grown in sustainable forests. The logging and manufacturing processes are expected to conform to the environmental regulations of the country of origin.

Orders: please contact Bookpoint Ltd, 130 Park Drive, Abingdon, Oxon OX14 4SE. Telephone: (44) 01235 827720. Fax: (44) 01235 400454. Lines are open 9.00–5.00, Monday to Saturday, with a 24-hour message answering service. Visit our website at www.hoddereducation.co.uk. Hodder Gibson can be contacted direct on: Tel: 0141 848 1609; Fax: 0141 889 6315; email: hoddergibson@hodder.co.uk

This collection first published in 2014 by
Hodder Gibson, an imprint of Hodder Education,
An Hachette UK Company
2a Christie Street
Paisley PA1 1NB

{BrightRED Hodder Gibson is grateful to Bright Red Publishing Ltd for collaborative work in preparation of this book and all SQA Past Paper, National 5 and Higher for CfE Model Paper titles 2014.

Typeset by PDQ Digital Media Solutions Ltd, Bungay, Suffolk NR35 1BY

Printed in the UK

A catalogue record for this title is available from the British Library

ISBN: 978-1-4718-3719-7

3 2 1

2015 2014

Introduction

Study Skills – what you need to know to pass exams!

Pause for thought

Many students might skip quickly through a page like this. After all, we all know how to revise. Do you really though?

Think about this:

"IF YOU ALWAYS DO WHAT YOU ALWAYS DO, YOU WILL ALWAYS GET WHAT YOU HAVE ALWAYS GOT."

Do you like the grades you get? Do you want to do better? If you get full marks in your assessment, then that's great! Change nothing! This section is just to help you get that little bit better than you already are.

There are two main parts to the advice on offer here. The first part highlights fairly obvious things but which are also very important. The second part makes suggestions about revision that you might not have thought about but which WILL help you.

Part 1

DOH! It's so obvious but …

Start revising in good time

Don't leave it until the last minute – this will make you panic.

Make a revision timetable that sets out work time AND play time.

Sleep and eat!

Obvious really, and very helpful. Avoid arguments or stressful things too – even games that wind you up. You need to be fit, awake and focused!

Know your place!

Make sure you know exactly **WHEN and WHERE** your exams are.

Know your enemy!

Make sure you know what to expect in the exam.

How is the paper structured?

How much time is there for each question?

What types of question are involved?

Which topics seem to come up time and time again?

Which topics are your strongest and which are your weakest?

Are all topics compulsory or are there choices?

Learn by DOING!

There is no substitute for past papers and practice papers – they are simply essential! Tackling this collection of papers and answers is exactly the right thing to be doing as your exams approach.

Part 2

People learn in different ways. Some like low light, some bright. Some like early morning, some like evening/night. Some prefer warm, some prefer cold. But everyone uses their BRAIN and the brain works when it is active. Passive learning – sitting gazing at notes – is the most INEFFICIENT way to learn anything. Below you will find tips and ideas for making our revision more effectice and maybe even more enjoyable. What follows gets your brain active, and active learning works!

Activity 1 – Stop and review

Step 1

When you have done no more than 5 minutes of revision reading STOP!

Step 2

Write a heading in your own words which sums up the topic you have been revising.

Step 3

Write a summary of what you have revised in no more than two sentences. Don't fool yourself by saying, "I know it, but I cannot put it into words". That just means you don't know it well enough. If you cannot write your summary, revise that section again, knowing that you must write a summary at the end of it. Many of you will have notebooks full of blue/black ink writing. Many of the pages will not be especially attractive or memorable so try to liven them up a bit with colour as you are reviewing and rewriting. **This is a great memory aid, and memory is the most important thing.**

Activity 2 – Use technology!

Why should everything be written down? Have you thought about "mental" maps, diagrams, cartoons and colour to help you learn? And rather than write down notes, why not record your revision material?

What about having a text message revision session with friends? Keep in touch with them to find out how and what they are revising and share ideas and questions.

Why not make a video diary where you tell the camera what you are doing, what you think you have learned and what you still have to do? No one has to see or hear it, but the process of having to organise your thoughts in a formal way to explain something is a very important learning practice.

Be sure to make use of electronic files. You could begin to summarise your class notes. Your typing might be slow, but it will get faster and the typed notes will be easier to read than the scribbles in your class notes. Try to add different fonts and colours to make your work stand out. You can easily Google relevant pictures, cartoons and diagrams which you can copy and paste to make your work more attractive and **MEMORABLE**.

Activity 3 – This is it. Do this and you will know lots!

Step 1

In this task you must be very honest with yourself! Find the SQA syllabus for your subject (www.sqa.org.uk). Look at how it is broken down into main topics called MANDATORY knowledge. That means stuff you MUST know.

Step 2

BEFORE you do ANY revision on this topic, write a list of everything that you already know about the subject. It might be quite a long list but you only need to write it once. It shows you all the information that is already in your long-term memory so you know what parts you do not need to revise!

Step 3

Pick a chapter or section from your book or revision notes. Choose a fairly large section or a whole chapter to get the most out of this activity.

With a buddy, use Skype, Facetime, Twitter or any other communication you have, to play the game "If this is the answer, what is the question?". For example, if you are revising Geography and the answer you provide is "meander", your buddy would have to make up a question like "What is the word that describes a feature of a river where it flows slowly and bends often from side to side?".

Make up 10 "answers" based on the content of the chapter or section you are using. Give this to your buddy to solve while you solve theirs.

Step 4

Construct a wordsearch of at least 10 X 10 squares. You can make it as big as you like but keep it realistic. Work together with a group of friends. Many apps allow you to make wordsearch puzzles online. The words and phrases can go in any direction and phrases can be split. Your puzzle must only contain facts linked to the topic you are revising. Your task is to find 10 bits of information to hide in your puzzle, but you must not repeat information that you used in Step 3. DO NOT show where the words are. Fill up empty squares with random letters. Remember to keep a note of where your answers are hidden but do not show your friends. When you have a complete puzzle, exchange it with a friend to solve each other's puzzle.

Step 5

Now make up 10 questions (not "answers" this time) based on the same chapter used in the previous two tasks. Again, you must find NEW information that you have not yet used. Now it's getting hard to find that new information! Again, give your questions to a friend to answer.

Step 6

As you have been doing the puzzles, your brain has been actively searching for new information. Now write a NEW LIST that contains only the new information you have discovered when doing the puzzles. Your new list is the one to look at repeatedly for short bursts over the next few days. Try to remember more and more of it without looking at it. After a few days, you should be able to add words from your second list to your first list as you increase the information in your long-term memory.

FINALLY! Be inspired...

Make a list of different revision ideas and beside each one write **THINGS I HAVE** tried, **THINGS I WILL** try and **THINGS I MIGHT** try. Don't be scared of trying something new.

And remember – "FAIL TO PREPARE AND PREPARE TO FAIL!"

Higher French

The course

The Higher French course aims to enable you to develop the ability to:

- read, listen, talk and write in French
- understand and use French
- apply your knowledge and understanding of the language.

The course offers the opportunity to develop detailed language skills in the real-life contexts of society, learning, employability and culture.

How the course is graded

The course assessment will take the form of a performance and a written exam:

- The performance will be a presentation and discussion with your teacher, which will be recorded and marked by your teacher. This is out of 30, and makes up 30% of your final mark.
- The written exam will be sat in May. This book will help you practise for the exam.

The exams

Reading and Directed Writing

- exam time: 1 hour 40 minutes

Reading

- total marks: 30
- weighting in final grade: 30%
- what you have to do: read a passage of about 600 words, and answer questions about it in English, including an overall purpose question for 20 marks; translate an extract from the passage of about 40 words into English for 10 marks.

Directed Writing

- total marks: 10
- weighting in final grade: 10%
- what you have to do: write 120–150 words in French describing a visit you made, or an experience you had, in a French speaking country.

Listening and Personal Response Writing

- exam time: 60 minutes
- total marks: 30
- weighting in final grade: 30%
- what you have to do: Section 1 (20 marks): listen to a presentation in French, and answer questions about it in English; then listen to a conversation In French, and answer questions about it in English. Section 2 (10 marks): write 120–150 words in

French as a personal response to the topic discussed in the conversation: there will be three specific questions to be addressed.

How to improve your mark!

Reading

- Read the whole passage, then pick out the key points. Detailed answers are generally required, so pay particular attention to words like assez, très, trop, vraiment and to negatives. Make sure you get the details of numbers, days, times etc. right.
- Use the line numbers above each question to guide you as to where to look for the answer.
- Take care when using dictionaries where a word has more than one meaning. Learn to choose the correct meaning from a list of meanings in a dictionary, and get in the habit of going beyond the headword. Often you will find the whole phrase you are looking for further down the entry.
- Try to answer the specific wording of the question, but do not give a word-for-word translation of the text as a response to the reading comprehension questions, as this often results in an answer which is not in correct English.
- When responding to the questions in the Reading papers, you should be guided by the number of points awarded for each question. You should give as much detail in your answer as you have understood, but should not put down everything which is in the original text, as you are wasting time. The question itself usually indicates the amount of information required by stating in bold, e.g. 'State **two** of them'. If the question says 'Give **any two**', there are more than two possibilities, so choose the two you are happiest with and stick to them.
- The last question before the translation asks you to look at the passage as a whole, then answer a question and provide evidence to back up your answer. It is important to start your answer with your opinion, then select pieces of text from the passage to back up your answer, giving an English version of what is in the passage.
- Look closely at each word in each section of the translation passage, and pay particular attention to the articles and tenses used. Make sure you include each word in your translation (although translation is not word for word!) Look at marking schemes for translations to give you an idea of what a good translation should look like.

Directed Writing

- Have a quick look at the two choices for writing, and go for the one for which your prepared material will give you most support.

- Consider, carefully, the wording of each bullet point, and make sure any learned material that you use is relevant and appropriate to the bullet point. Make sure you address each part of the first bullet point, and that you are answering the questions asked.

- Use your dictionary only to check the accuracy of what you have written (spelling, genders etc.), not to create and invent new sentences.

- Don't write pieces that are too lengthy, you only need 120–150 words. So stick to 30–40 words per bullet point.

- Be aware of the extended criteria to be used in assessing performances in Writing (included on pages 114–116 and pages 117–119 of this book!) so that you know what's required to achieve the good and very good categories in terms of content, accuracy, and range and variety of language.

- Ensure that your handwriting is legible (particularly when writing in French) and distinguish clearly between rough notes and what you wish to be considered as final answers. Make sure you score out your notes!

- You should bear the following points in mind:

  - There are four bullet points to answer: they are not really predictable and vary from year to year, but certain things come up regularly.

  - Each of the four bullet points should have between 30 and 40 words to address it properly.

  - You will be assessed on how well you have answered the points, and on the accuracy of your language.

  - If you miss out or fail to address a bullet point correctly, the most you can get is six marks.

  - For a mark of good or very good, you should have some complex language such as longer, varied sentences, adjectives and conjunctions.

Listening

- Your listening skills will improve most with practice. So use the Listening sections in this book several times to get used to the format of the exam.

- Read the questions carefully before the first listening and use them as a means of anticipating the sort of information you will need to extract from the text.

- Not giving enough detail is still a major reason for candidates losing marks. Many answers are correct as far as they go, but don't have enough detail to score marks. The same rules as for Reading apply. Give as much detail as possible in your answers and don't lose marks by writing down numbers, prepositions and question words inaccurately.

- You hear each of the two Listening texts twice only, so make use of the gap between the two recordings to check which specific details you still need for your answers, so your listening is focused.

- Make sure you're able to give accurate answers through confident knowledge of numbers, common adjectives, weather expressions, prepositions and question words, so that some of the 'easier' points of information are not lost through lack of sufficiently accurate details.

- When responding to the questions in the Listening papers, be guided by the number of points awarded for each question, and by the wording of the question. You should give as much detail in your answer as you have understood, but should not write down everything you hear. The question itself usually indicates the amount of information required by stating in bold, e.g. 'Give **2** of them'.

- Be sure to put a line through any notes you have made!

Personal Response Writing

- Make sure you read the stimulus questions carefully and adapt any learned material you use so it's relevant to the aspects contained in them.

- There are three questions to be answered and you must answer them all, at roughly the same length. Aim for 40 to 50 words for each of them.

- Don't be tempted to rewrite an answer you have written on the topic previously: you have to be sure your answer is relevant to the questions put to you.

Good luck!

Remember that the rewards for passing Higher French are well worth it! Your pass will help you get the future you want for yourself. In the exam, be confident in your own ability. If you're not sure how to answer a question, trust your instincts and just give it a go anyway – keep calm and don't panic! GOOD LUCK!

National Qualifications
SPECIMEN ONLY

SQ17/H/11

**French
Reading**

Date — Not applicable

Duration — 1 hour and 40 minutes

Total marks — 30

Attempt ALL questions.

Write your answers clearly, in **English**, in the Reading answer booklet provided. In the answer booklet you must clearly identify the question number you are attempting.

You may use a French dictionary.

Use **blue** or **black** ink.

There is a separate question and answer booklet for Directed Writing. You must complete your answer for Directed Writing in the question and answer booklet for Directed Writing.

Before leaving the examination room you must give your Reading answer booklet and your Directed Writing question and answer booklet to the Invigilator; if you do not, you may lose all the marks for this paper.

Total marks — 30

Attempt ALL questions

Read the whole article carefully and then answer, in English, ALL the questions that follow.

In this article, the writer discusses holidays.

Les vacances - nécessité ou luxe?

Certains disent que partir en vacances, soit à l'étranger, soit dans son propre pays, est une vraie nécessité. D'autres pensent que c'est un luxe qu'on ne peut pas se permettre de nos jours.

Malgré l'augmentation du coût de la vie, pas question pour les Français d'y renoncer
5 parce qu'ils adorent partir en vacances. Chaque été un grand nombre se met en route pour quitter les villes et s'échapper de la vie quotidienne. Ils partent non seulement pendant les grandes vacances, mais aussi en hiver, et même pour des séjours de courte durée.

Pourquoi partir en vacances?

10 Selon le psychologue, Martin Lescaux, on a besoin de partir en vacances pour toutes sortes de raisons. Tout d'abord, il est nécessaire de s'éloigner du bureau. Tant de gens sont obligés de faire des heures supplémentaires, et par conséquent ils rentrent épuisés à la maison où ils doivent encore s'occuper des enfants. Puis, on recommence la même routine le lendemain.

15 Alors, partir en vacances est une bonne occasion de se reposer, d'oublier la routine et de faire ce qu'on veut. Si on reste à la maison, on risque de finir par faire les tâches ménagères.

Quelles sortes de vacances attirent les Français depuis la crise économique?

Pour beaucoup de Français, les projets de vacances ont beaucoup changé. Mais, ils n'ont
20 pas besoin d'aller très loin, et chose étonnante: la visite d'usines, de centrales nucléaires et de fromageries devient de plus en plus populaire. Il y a toujours quelque chose de nouveau à découvrir, tout près de chez soi.

Si on a la chance d'habiter pas trop loin des montagnes, il est toujours possible de passer une journée au ski. Mais, Jérôme Bertillon, propriétaire d'un hôtel de montagne, nous
25 explique:

<< Les vacances à la montagne ce n'est pas que le ski. Moi, j'ai des clients qui pratiquent une variété d'activités sportives pendant la journée, mais le soir ce qui les attirent c'est de se retrouver entre amis ou en famille, auprès de la cheminée à chanter ou à discuter avec une boisson chaude à la main.

30 En plus, il y a d'autres raisons de visiter la montagne. N'oubliez pas que respirer l'air frais de la montagne vous fera beaucoup de bien, que vous choisissiez des activités physiques ou non! Après tout, qui ne veut pas se réveiller le matin avec une vue magnifique sur les montagnes? >>

Par contre, l'été, plus de 35 millions de Français partent en vacances en même temps sur
35 les côtes de la Méditerranée ou de l'Atlantique. Pour beaucoup de vacanciers, revenir de vacances bronzés est un signe de vacances réussies. Les seuls inconvénients sont qu'on peut passer des heures bloqué en voiture à cause des bouchons sur les autoroutes, et il va sans dire qu'on est tellement serré à la plage qu'il est souvent difficile de trouver un endroit pour s'allonger sur le sable.

40 **Le tourisme vert**

<u>Cependant, l'année dernière, beaucoup de Français ont choisi de passer leurs vacances à la campagne qui a tant de choses à offrir. Par exemple, on peut passer des journées au bord d'une rivière à pêcher ou même faire une promenade en vélo en forêt tout en découvrant l'histoire de la région.</u>

45 En fait, le «tourisme vert» est très à la mode en ce moment, et beaucoup de monde choisit de louer des cabanes en pleine forêt ou bien de dormir dans les arbres parce que les prix sont beaucoup plus raisonnables par rapport aux prix qu'on paie dans un hôtel de luxe.

Le psychologue, Martin Lescaux, dit, « Dans un monde où l'on oublie l'impact de l'homme
50 sur l'environnement, cela donne l'occasion de se trouver plus près de la nature où il faut penser aux animaux et à la beauté qui nous entourent.»

En conclusion, une chose est certaine – en dépit de la crise économique les Français n'ont aucune intention de renoncer aux vacances! En tout cas, pas pour l'instant!

MARKS

Questions

Re-read lines 4—8

1. The opening of the article states that the increase in the cost of living has not had an effect on the attitude of French people towards holidays.

    What evidence is there of this?   State any **two** examples.   2

Re-read lines 10—17

2. According to the psychologist, Martin Lescaux:

    (a) Why do people need to go on holiday? State any **three** reasons   3

    (b) Why is it not a good idea to stay at home?   1

Re-read lines 18—22

3. The economic crisis has had an impact on holiday choices.

    (a) In what way have the holiday plans of many French people changed?   1

    (b) What is surprising about this change?   1

MARKS

Re-read lines 23—33

4. The writer discusses ski holidays.

    (a) According to Jérôme Bertillon, what are the main attractions for holidaymakers in the mountains? Give any **two** details.   **2**

    (b) What other reasons does he give for the popularity of a mountain holiday?   **2**

Re-read lines 34—39

5. Many French people choose to spend their summer holidays on the coast.

    (a) What do some people see as a sign of a successful holiday?   **1**

    (b) What are the main disadvantages of this type of holiday?   **2**

Re-read lines 45—51

6. The article discusses "Eco tourism".

    What attracts people to this type of holiday? State any **three** reasons.   **3**

7. Now consider the article as a whole.

    Does the author give the impression that holidays are a necessity or a luxury? Give details from the text to justify your answer.   **2**

8. Translate into English:

    "Cependant, ... de la région." (*lines 41—44*)   **10**

[END OF SPECIMEN QUESTION PAPER]

H

Mark

National
Qualifications
SPECIMEN ONLY

SQ17/H/02

**French
Directed Writing**

Date — Not applicable

Duration — 1 hour and 40 minutes

Fill in these boxes and read what is printed below.

Full name of centre

Town

Forename(s)

Surname

Number of seat

Date of birth

| Day | Month | Year |

Scottish candidate number

Total marks — 10

Choose ONE scenario on *Page two* and write your answer clearly, in **French**, in the space provided in this booklet. You must clearly identify the scenario number you are attempting.

You may use a French dictionary.

Additional space for answers is provided at the end of this booklet.

Use **blue** or **black** ink.

There is a separate answer booklet for Reading. You must complete your answers for Reading in the answer booklet for Reading.

Before leaving the examination room you must give this Directed Writing question and answer booklet and your Reading answer booklet to the Invigilator; if you do not, you may lose all the marks for this paper.

Total marks — 10

Choose **one** of the following two scenarios.

SCENARIO 1: Employability

> You have recently returned from France, where you have spent the summer working.
>
> On your return, you have been asked to write an account of your experiences to try to encourage other pupils to do the same thing.

You must include the following information and **you should try to add** other relevant details:

- What your job was **and** what you thought of the people you worked with
- What you had to do in your job
- What you liked/disliked about the job
- If you would recommend such an experience to others

You should write approximately 120—150 words.

OR

SCENARIO 2: Culture

> Last December you went with a group of students from your school/college to a town in France for a few days. While you were there you went to a Christmas market.
>
> On your return you were asked to write a report, **in French**, of your visit.

You must include the following information and **you should try to add** other relevant details:

- Where you stayed **and** what you thought of the accommodation
- What you did at the market
- What you liked/disliked most about the experience
- How you plan to keep in touch with your new friends in the future

You should write approximately 120—150 words.

ANSWER SPACE

MARKS | DO NOT WRITE IN THIS MARGIN

Scenario number

_____

_____

_____

_____

_____

_____

_____

_____

_____

_____

_____

_____

_____

_____

_____

_____

_____

_____

_____

_____

_____

_____

_____

_____

ANSWER SPACE (continued)

MARKS | DO NOT WRITE IN THIS MARGIN

ANSWER SPACE (continued)

ANSWER SPACE (continued)

[END OF SPECIMEN QUESTION PAPER]

MARKS

ADDITIONAL SPACE FOR ANSWERS

MARKS   DO NOT WRITE IN THIS MARGIN

ADDITIONAL SPACE FOR ANSWERS

H

National
Qualifications
SPECIMEN ONLY

Mark

SQ17/H/03

**French
Listening and Writing**

Date — Not applicable

Duration — 1 hour

Fill in these boxes and read what is printed below.

Full name of centre

Town

Forename(s)

Surname

Number of seat

Date of birth
Day   Month   Year

Scottish candidate number

Total marks — 30

SECTION 1 — LISTENING — 20 marks.

You will hear two items in French. **Before you hear each item, you will have one minute to study the question.** You will hear each item twice, with an interval of one minute between playings. You will then have time to answer the questions before hearing the next item. Write your answers clearly, in **English**, in the spaces provided.

SECTION 2 — WRITING — 10 marks.

Write your answer clearly, in **French**, in the space provided.

Attempt ALL questions. You may use a French dictionary.

Additional space for answers is provided at the end of this booklet. If you use this space you must clearly identify the question number you are attempting.

You are not allowed to leave the examination room until the end of the test.

Use **blue** or **black** ink.

Before leaving the examination room you must give this booklet to the Invigilator; if you do not, you may lose all the marks for this paper.

MARKS | DO NOT WRITE IN THIS MARGIN

SECTION 1 — LISTENING — 20 marks

Attempt ALL questions

Item 1

You listen to a news bulletin about the French government's plans to change the school day.

(a) Why does the French government want to make changes to the school day?   **1**

_____

(b) (i) How much time do French secondary school pupils spend in class?   **1**

_____

(ii) In what way do their results compare to those in other countries?   **1**

_____

(c) What changes does the government plan to make to the school day? State any **two** things.   **2**

_____

_____

(d) What benefits would there be for pupils? State any **two** things.   **2**

_____

_____

(e) Overall, which statement best describes the speaker's opinion about the proposed changes. Tick (✓) the correct statement.   **1**

They will make no difference.	
They will improve performance.	
Pupils will waste a lot of time.	

MARKS | DO NOT WRITE IN THIS MARGIN

Item 2

Pierre speaks to Audrey about school and her plans for the future.

(a) Audrey has a very heavy workload this year. What is the result of this?   **1**

_____

(b) (i) State **two** reasons why Audrey loves studying languages.   **2**

_____

_____

(ii) Why does she prefer Spanish? Give **two** details.   **2**

_____

_____

(c) (i) What is Audrey's dream job?   **1**

_____

(ii) Why is it so difficult to get this kind of job?   **1**

_____

(iii) What are employers looking for in terms of language qualifications?   **1**

_____

(d) (i) What experience has Audrey had working with children?   **2**

_____

(ii) Why does Audrey think she would enjoy being a teacher?   **2**

_____

_____

SECTION 2 — WRITING — 10 marks

Audrey nous a parlé de son expérience au lycée et de ses projets d'avenir.

Penses-tu comme Audrey que les langues sont importantes pour l'avenir?

Est-ce-que ton lycée/collège te prépare bien pour le monde du travail?

As-tu des projets précis pour le futur?

Ecris 120—150 mots en français pour exprimer tes idées.

ANSWER SPACE FOR SECTION 2 (continued)

[END OF SPECIMEN QUESTION PAPER]

ADDITIONAL SPACE FOR ANSWERS

MARKS | DO NOT WRITE IN THIS MARGIN

Page six

ADDITIONAL SPACE FOR ANSWERS

National
Qualifications
SPECIMEN ONLY

SQ17/H/13

**French
Listening Transcript**

Date — Not applicable

Duration — 1 hour

This paper must not be seen by any candidate.

The material overleaf is provided for use in an emergency only (eg the recording or equipment proving faulty) or where permission has been given in advance by SQA for the material to be read to candidates with additional support needs. The material must be read exactly as printed.

Transcript — Higher

> **Instructions to reader(s):**
>
> For each item, read the English **once**, then read the French **twice**, with an interval of 1 minute between the two readings. On completion of the second reading, pause for the length of time indicated in brackets after the item, to allow the candidates to write their answers.
>
> Where special arrangements have been agreed in advance to allow the reading of the material, those sections marked **(f)** should be read by a female speaker and those marked **(m)** by a male; those sections marked **(t)** should be read by the teacher.

(t)   **Item 1**

You listen to a news bulletin about the French government's plans to change the school day.

You now have one minute to study the questions for Item 1.

(m/f)   Selon le gouvernement français, l'emploi du temps dans les écoles doit changer parce que le système actuel n'est pas efficace.

Et voilà pourquoi. Les jeunes Français passent plus de temps en classe que les autres élèves européens. Pour beaucoup d'élèves, la journée scolaire commence à 8 heures et ne finit qu'à 18 heures. Ça veut dire que dans le secondaire, les élèves peuvent passer jusqu'à 40 heures de cours par semaine à l'école.

Et pourtant, bien qu'ils travaillent plus, les élèves Français n'ont pas de meilleurs résultats scolaires que leurs voisins européens, comme, par exemple, les élèves espagnols, allemands ou britanniques.

Donc, le gouvernement veut introduire un nouveau système, où on va avoir une journée plus courte. Il y aurait un maximum de sept heures de cours par jour et la journée finirait à 17 heures.

Cela permettrait aux jeunes Français de se concentrer en classe et d'être plus attentifs parce qu'ils seraient moins fatigués.

Ils auraient aussi la possibilité de faire du sport et pratiquer des activités parascolaires et d'avoir plus de temps pour se détendre et se reposer.

Mais, pour créer des journées plus courtes on va réduire les vacances d'été à 7 semaines au lieu des 9 semaines actuelles.

Ainsi, les élèves auraient moins de temps pour oublier le travail scolaire!

(2 minutes)

(t) **Item 2**

Pierre speaks to Audrey about school and her plans for the future.

You now have one minute to study the questions for Item 2.

(m) **Audrey, tu as beaucoup de travail à faire cette année?**

(f) Ah oui, j'ai un emploi du temps très chargé cette année. J'ai l'impression que je travaille tout le temps en ce moment, donc je n'ai pas beaucoup de temps pour faire ce que je veux.

(m) **Qu'est-ce que tu fais comme matières cette année?**

(f) Les langues étrangères, bien sûr. J'adore bavarder, que ce soit en français, anglais ou espagnol . . . Je dois avouer que mes profs de langues sont tous géniaux. Leurs cours sont toujours intéressants. Mais, je suppose que ma langue préférée c'est l'espagnol. Dans cette classe, il faut seulement parler espagnol. Ce règlement me plaît parce que, comme ça, on progresse beaucoup plus vite! Les langues sont très importantes à mon avis.

(m) **Pourquoi penses-tu que les langues sont importantes?**

(f) Si on veut vraiment connaître la culture et les gens d'un autre pays, il est essentiel de parler la langue du pays.

(m) **Qu'est-ce-que tu veux faire à l'avenir?**

(f) Mon rêve serait d'être interprète et de travailler au parlement européen à Strasbourg . . . Cependant, je suis réaliste. Je sais qu' il y a beaucoup de compétition car beaucoup d'étudiants à l'université sont bilingues. Et de nos jours, il me semble que les employeurs recherchent des langues un peu différentes comme le chinois . . . mais bon, si je n'arrive pas à devenir interprète, j'ai toujours l'option de devenir prof de langues . . .

(m) **Oh là là, moi, je ne pourrais jamais devenir prof ! Pourquoi veux- tu devenir prof?**

(f) J'adore travailler avec les enfants. Chaque été je travaille comme monitrice en colonie de vacances dans le sud de la France. Je dois organiser des activités créatives pour les enfants. Je trouve ça très intéressant. J'ai aussi un petit boulot de babysitter que je fais depuis l'âge de quatorze ans.

(m) **Mais tu penses que le métier de prof te plaîrait ?**

(f) Oui depuis toute petite, j'ai toujours voulu être prof parce que tout le monde dans ma famille est prof . . . mon père est prof de maths et ma mère prof de dessin! Et malgré le stress, je sais qu'ils adorent leur travail . . . En plus, les profs ont de très longues vacances!

(2 minutes)

(t) **End of test.**

Now look over your answers.

[END OF SPECIMEN TRANSCRIPT]

Model Paper 1

Whilst this Model Practice Paper has been specially commissioned by Hodder Gibson for use as practice for the Higher (for Curriculum for Excellence) exams, the key reference document remains the SQA Specimen Paper 2014.

National Qualifications
MODEL PAPER 1

French
Reading

Duration — 1 hour and 40 minutes

Total marks — 30

Attempt ALL questions.

Write your answers clearly, in **English**, in the Reading answer booklet. In the answer booklet you must clearly identify the question number you are attempting.

You may use a French dictionary.

Use **blue** or **black** ink.

There is a separate question and answer booklet for Directed Writing. You must complete your answer for Directed Writing in the question and answer booklet for Directed Writing.

Before leaving the examination room you must give your Reading answer booklet and your Directed Writing question and answer booklet to the Invigilator; if you do not, you may lose all the marks for this paper.

Total marks — 30

Attempt ALL questions

Read the whole article carefully and then answer, in English, ALL the questions that follow.

In this article, the writer discusses the situation of people whose parents and grandparents emigrated to France from its former colonies in North Africa.

Les maghrébins en France

Le Maghreb compte environ 90 millions d'habitants répartis partout dans le Nord de l'Afrique. La plupart de la population se rencontre sur les plaines de l'océan Atlantique et de la mer Méditerranée. Mais après des années d'immigration en France, il existe aussi une grande population de maghrébins en France. On estimait en 2012 que les personnes d'origine
5   maghrébine sur 3 générations (immigrés, enfants et petits-enfants d'immigrés) étaient plus de 3,5 millions, soit environ 6% de la population française. Pour la plupart ces maghrébins sont des musulmans.

Depuis la Révolution de 1789 et la formation de la République française, la laïcité, c'est-à-dire la séparation de l'église et l'état, a été très importante pour les Français. Le gouvernement français a
10   introduit en 1905 une loi sur la laïcité qui concernait la chrétienté et le judaïsme, les réligions importantes dans la France à cette époque. Aujourd'hui la concentration de la presse et des politiciens est sur l'Islam. De nos jours, pendant trente ans au moins, la religion musulmane a connu un fort rejet par les pouvoirs publics. Le gouvernement national a souvent fermé les yeux sur les très grands problèmes occasionnés par des politiciens locaux pour l'Islam et les
15   musulmans.

En plus, le modèle d'intégration à la française n'a pas permis aux jeunes générations issues de l'immigration maghrébine de prendre la place qui leur revient dans la construction d'une société nouvelle. Mais n'oublions pas ce qu'a dit Karim Benzema, footballeur né a Lyon en 1987 de parents d'origine algérienne, qui a déclaré : " L'Algérie c'est le pays de mes parents, c'est dans
20   mon cœur, mais sportivement, je jouerai en équipe de France."

La République française a beaucoup changé à cause de facteurs divers, comme l'Union Européenne et les profondes transformations de son économie. Dès la fin des années soixante-dix ces processus ont mené à la disparition du caractère populaire de la plupart des banlieues, à cause du
25   regroupement familial immigré et du départ des populations européennes. C'était le début de la ghettoïsation et de la concentration ethnique. Journaliste Remy Desmoulins raconte: *"Les ruptures sociales sont maintenant très évidentes: les gens aisés avec leurs bons emplois réclament plus de liberté et d'indépendance, alors que les pauvres, ou sans emploi ou qui travaillent pour le SMIC** ont surtout besoin de sécurité et de solidarité. Les politiques modernes ne touchent plus la masse
30   des gens. C'est ainsi que se sont enracinés, dans les quartiers les plus pauvres, l'extrême-droite raciste et l'islamisme radical."

Alors, quoi faire? Il faudra recréer de l'espoir. Il nous faudra nommer les problèmes dans notre société et trouver des solutions qui peuvent améliorer concrètement le sort des gens qui souffrent dans les ghettos. Il faudra réduire la fracture culturelle entre les maghrébins et la société française. La République peut rattraper le temps perdu. Elle doit arrêter de renvoyer l'islam et les musulmans
35   vers une sorte de vie de seconde classe. Les pouvoirs publics doivent permettre aux musulmans d'occuper une place honorable dans la société française. Ils doivent parler aux musulmans de leurs problèmes spécifiques : la construction de mosquées, la provision de lieux pour leurs cimetières, les problèmes de la distribution et du contrôle de la viande halal, etc.

Mais, parallèlement à ce programme, les musulmans doivent admettre que la République contrôle
40   le droit, et affirmer que les citoyens de confession musulmane partagent l'essentiel des valeurs qui fondent le système juridique de la France. Ils doivent reconnaître pleinement l'égalité entre les femmes et les hommes. Cela permettra aux maghrébins d'être mieux acceptés par la République et par la société française, et permettra à la république de pouvoir s'appuyer sur ces « nouveaux » citoyens.

* le SMIC - minimum wage

Page two

MARKS

Questions

Re-read lines 1–7

1. The opening of the article gives some background information about the Maghreb and its inhabitants.

   What fact are we given about most of the immigrants to France?   1

   Re-read lines 8–15

2. The paragraph discusses the separation of church and state in France, and the problems this is now causing.

   (a) What has been the change of emphasis since the 1905 law? Give details.   2

   (b) What has been the problem over the last 30 years? Give details.   3

   Re-read lines 15–20

3. The writer discusses the French idea of integration.

   (a) What problem is this now causing?   1

   (b) In what way does Karim Benzema describe his nationality? Give details.   2

   Re-read lines 21–30

4. We are told about the big changes which have taken place in French society since the 1970s in particular.

   (a) Several developments have occurred through these changes. State any **two** of them.   2

   (b) What has the loss of faith in modern politics led to?   2

   Re-read lines 31–38

5. The author suggests ways to improve things.

   (a) What should the French try to reduce?   1

   (b) Several concrete suggestions are made to help address the needs of Muslims. Give details of any **two** of them.   2

MARKS

Re-read lines 39-44

6. The author suggests two ways Muslims could help improve the situation. Give details.   **2**

7. Now consider the article as a whole. Does the author give the impression that the situation is irretrievable? Give details from the text to justify your answer.   **2**

8. Translate into English:

"Les ruptures … solidarité." (*lines 26–28*)   **10**

[END OF MODEL QUESTION PAPER]

National
Qualifications
MODEL PAPER 1

French
Directed Writing

Duration — 1 hour and 40 minutes

Fill in these boxes and read what is printed below.

Full name of centre

Town

Forename(s)

Surname

Number of seat

Date of birth
Day   Month   Year

Scottish candidate number

Total marks — 10

Choose ONE scenario on *Page two* and write your answer clearly, in **French**, in the space provided in this booklet. You must clearly identify the scenario number you are attempting.

You may use a French dictionary.

Use **blue** or **black** ink.

There is a separate answer booklet for Reading. You must complete your answers for Reading in the answer booklet for Reading.

Before leaving the examination room you must give this Directed Writing question and answer booklet and your Reading answer booklet to the Invigilator; if you do not, you may lose all the marks for this paper.

Total marks — 10

Choose **one** of the following two scenarios.

SCENARIO 1: Society

> You have recently returned from France, where you have spent three weeks staying with a French friend.
>
> On your return, you have been asked to write an account of your experiences to try to encourage other pupils to do the same thing.

You must include the following information and **you should try to add** other relevant details:

*   Where you went **and** how you got there

*   What you did while you were there

*   How you got on with the family

*   If you would recommend such an experience to others

You should write approximately 120—150 words.

OR

SCENARIO 2: Employability

> Last year you went with a group of students from your school/college to a town in France for a week's work experience. While you were there you had a job found for you.
>
> On your return you were asked to write a report, **in French**, of your visit.

You must include the following information and **you should try to add** other relevant details:

*   Where you stayed **and** what you thought of the accommodation
*   What you did at work
*   What you liked/disliked most about the experience
*   How you plan to develop the links you made there

You should write approximately 120—150 words.

ANSWER SPACE

Scenario number

ANSWER SPACE (continued)

MARKS | DO NOT WRITE IN THIS MARGIN

ANSWER SPACE (continued)

MARKS | DO NOT WRITE IN THIS MARGIN

ANSWER SPACE (continued)

[END OF MODEL QUESTION PAPER]

MARKS DO NOT WRITE IN THIS MARGIN

ADDITIONAL SPACE FOR ANSWERS

MARKS

ADDITIONAL SPACE FOR ANSWERS

National
Qualifications
MODEL PAPER 1

French
Listening and Writing

Duration — 1 hour

Fill in these boxes and read what is printed below.

Full name of centre   Town

Forename(s)   Surname   Number of seat

Date of birth
Day   Month   Year   Scottish candidate number

Total marks — 30

SECTION 1 — LISTENING — 20 marks

You will hear two items in French. **Before you hear each item, you will have one minute to study the questions.** You will hear each item twice, with an interval of one minute between playings. You will then have time to answer the questions before hearing the next item. Write your answers clearly, in **English**, in the spaces provided.

SECTION 2 — WRITING — 10 marks

Write your answer clearly, in **French**, in the space provided.

Attempt ALL questions. You may use a French dictionary.

Additional space for answers is provided at the end of this booklet. If you use this space, you must clearly identify the question number you are attempting.

You are not allowed to leave the examination room until the end of the test.

Use **blue** or **black** ink.

Before leaving the examination room you must give your answer booklet to the Invigilator; if you do not, you may lose all the marks for this paper.

HODDER GIBSON
LEARN MORE

	MARKS	DO NOT WRITE IN THIS MARGIN

SECTION 1 — LISTENING — 20 marks

Attempt ALL questions

Item 1

You listen to a French careers adviser talking about going to university.

(a) What is the main reason for people going to university? — **1**

_____

(b) What will this allow them to do? — **1**

_____

(c) What other reason do some people give for going to university? — **1**

_____

(d) The speaker talks about how university is different from school.

    (i) State any **one** difference. — **1**

    _____

    (ii) What does the speaker say to reassure his audience? — **1**

    _____

(e) What **two** options does the speaker say might be suitable for some students? — **2**

_____

_____

(f) Overall, which statement best describes the speaker's opinion about going to university? Tick (✓) the correct statement. — **1**

He says it is not for everyone	
He thinks it can be challenging but worthwhile if you are ready	
He encourages all the audience to take the opportunity of going to university	

MARKS | DO NOT WRITE IN THIS MARGIN

Item 2

Marc talks about his first two years at university.

(a) What is the main reason he gives for choosing to go to university?   1

_____

(b) Where does he intend to work when he has finished?   1

_____

(c) He talks about what is important to him.

    (i) What is his main aim at university?   1

_____

    (ii) What does he think the main role of a university should be?   1

_____

(d) What does the university organise to help first year students?   1

_____

(e) Why does he think this is necessary? Give details.   2

_____

(f) What alarming statistic does he mention?   1

_____

(g) What did he do to prepare himself for university? State any **two** things.   2

_____

(h) What strengths did he discover he has?   1

_____

(i) State any **one** thing his school did to prepare him for university.   1

_____

MARKS | DO NOT WRITE IN THIS MARGIN

SECTION 2 — WRITING — 10 marks

Marc nous a parlé de son expérience à l'université.

Penses-tu à aller à l'université? Pourquoi?

Est-ce-que ton lycée/collège te prépare bien pour le futur et les études?

Que veulent-ils faire, tes amis?

Ecris 120—150 mots en français pour exprimer tes idées.

MARKS | DO NOT WRITE IN THIS MARGIN

ANSWER SPACE FOR SECTION 2 (continued)

[END OF MODEL QUESTION PAPER]

MARKS | DO NOT WRITE IN THIS MARGIN

ADDITIONAL SPACE FOR ANSWERS

MARKS

DO NOT WRITE IN THIS MARGIN

ADDITIONAL SPACE FOR ANSWERS

Page seven

National Qualifications
MODEL PAPER 1

French
Listening Transcript

Duration — 1 hour

This paper must not be seen by any candidate.

The material overleaf is provided for use in an emergency only (eg the recording or equipment proving faulty) or where permission has been given in advance by SQA for the material to be read to candidates with additional support needs. The material must be read exactly as printed.

HODDER
GIBSON
LEARN MORE

Transcript — Higher

Instructions to reader(s):

For each item, read the English **once**, then read the French **twice**, with an interval of 1 minute between the two readings. On completion of the second reading, pause for the length of time indicated in brackets after the item, to allow the candidates to write their answers.

Where special arrangements have been agreed in advance to allow the reading of the material, those sections marked **(f)** should be read by a female speaker and those marked **(m)** by a male; those sections marked **(t)** should be read by the teacher.

(t)   **Item 1**

You listen to a French careers adviser talking about going to university.

You now have one minute to study the questions for Item 1.

(m/f) Les gens décident d'aller à l'université pour de nombreuses raisons. Pour certaines personnes, l'obtention d'un certificat ou d'un diplôme est un point de départ pour trouver un emploi ou commencer une carrière. En fait, les études supérieures sont nécessaires pour de nombreuses carrières ou professions.

D'autres personnes considèrent que l'éducation est une partie importante de leur développement personnel. Aller à l'université donne l'occasion d'apprendre de nouvelles choses, de rencontrer de nouvelles personnes et de demander plus de soi grâce aux nouvelles expériences et aux nouvelles idées.

L'université est bien différente de l'école secondaire. La pression y est plus forte. On vous considère comme un adulte et vous êtes tenu responsable de vous-même. Aller à l'université peut aussi coïncider avec votre première expérience de vie seule ou loin de la maison. Si vous y allez, ça peut être difficile au début. Mais vous n'êtes pas seul. Toute personne qui quitte sa famille pour cette nouvelle expérience, vit la même chose.

Il est possible d'aller faire vos études à temps partiel pour trouver un équilibre entre les études et le travail et donc gagner de l'argent. Vous pouvez également considérer d'autres options comme l'éducation à distance pour vous permettre de compléter vos cours dès la maison.

Aller à l'université peut être difficile pour tous les étudiants. Avant de vous décider à faire une demande d'admission dans une université, vous devez vous assurer que c'est le bon moment pour poursuivre vos études.

(2 minutes)

(t) **Item 2**

Marc talks about his first two years at university.

You now have one minute to study the questions for Item 2.

(f) **Pour quelles raisons est-ce que vous allez à l'école?**

(m) Si tu n'as pas de diplôme, tu es limité. Je n'étais pas suffisamment qualifié pour trouver un bon emploi.

(f) **L'université est-elle alors bien nécessaire pour vous?**

(m) Eh bien, je veux travailler dans le monde de l'information. On peut être vraiment dire que l'enseignement supérieur est indispensable pour préparer les étudiants aux emplois de l'économie de l'information.

(f) **Qu'est-ce que vous désirez accomplir, donc ? La préparation pour l'emploi?**

(m) Tout simplement, je veux apprendre des choses. Quand le seul objectif de l'éducation est la production de diplômes plutôt que la promotion du savoir, le système oublie que: «Tous les hommes désirent naturellement savoir.»

(f) **Que fait votre université pour ceux qui ont plus de mal à suivre?**

(m) Les étudiants de 3ème année de licence ou de master viennent tutorer les étudiants de 1ère année en difficulté. Ceux-ci ont souvent du mal à travailler en groupe car ils ne voient pas pourquoi on doit partager les idées qui est pourtant l'un des fondamentaux de l'enseignement universitaire.

(f) **Beaucoup d'étudiants ne réussissent pas à leurs examens en première année. Quels en étaient les effets sur vous?**

(m) Sur les étudiants inscrits en première année dans certains sujets il y en a à peu près 25% qui réussissent un des concours, souvent avec un redoublement. Face à cette sélectivité, j'ai du devenir un excellent étudiant!

(f) **Qu'est-ce que vous saviez des demandes de la vie scolaire avant de venir en fac?**

(m) Je me suis informé de l'inscription aux cours, l'utilisation d'un ordinateur, la prise de note, la lecture, et les examens. J'ai fait bien de recherches.

(f) **Quelles sont vos forces?**

(m) J'ai la persévérance et la confiance nécessaires pour affronter les frustrations, et pour obtenir les informations dont j'ai besoin auprès des directeurs de l'école.

(f) **Comment est-ce que votre école vous a préparé pour réussir à l'université?**

(m) On m'a expliqué par exemple qu'il me serait difficile de réussir en licence de mathématiques si je n'ai jamais eu de bonnes notes dans cette discipline en classe de terminale. J'ai dû me très bien renseigner avant d'aller à l'université. En terminale j'ai pu venir visiter l'université.

(f) **Alors, merci de m'avoir parlé.**

(m) De rien, au revoir

(2 minutes)

(t) **End of test.**

Now look over your answers.

[END OF MODEL TRANSCRIPT]

Model Paper 2

Whilst this Model Practice Paper has been specially commissioned by Hodder Gibson for use as practice for the Higher (for Curriculum for Excellence) exams, the key reference document remains the SQA Specimen Paper 2014.

National
Qualifications
MODEL PAPER 2

French
Reading

Duration — 1 hour and 40 minutes

Total marks — 30

Attempt ALL questions.

Write your answers clearly, in **English**, in the Reading answer booklet. In the answer booklet you must clearly identify the question number you are attempting.

You may use a French dictionary.

Use **blue** or **black** ink.

There is a separate question and answer booklet for Directed Writing. You must complete your answer for Directed Writing in the question and answer booklet for Directed Writing.

Before leaving the examination room you must give your Reading answer booklet and your Directed Writing question and answer booklet to the Invigilator; if you do not, you may lose all the marks for this paper.

HODDER
GIBSON
LEARN MORE

Total marks — 30

Attempt ALL questions

Read the whole article carefully and then answer, in English, ALL the questions that follow.

In this article, the writer discusses the rise in PACS, or civil partnerships, in France.

Le PACS: un changement de direction

Quelles sont les conditions pour pouvoir se marier en France? Tout simplement il faut avoir dix-huit ans, être sain d'esprit, ne pas être déjà marié. Le mariage civil était jusqu'à 2013 aussi ouvert uniquement aux couples de sexe différent. Le mariage civil a lieu en général à la mairie, les bans* sont publiés dix jours au moins avant le mariage. Apres le mariage civil beaucoup de Français
5 fêtent aussi un mariage religieux. Dans le passé, les couples qui choisissaient de vivre ensemble sans se marier n'avaient pas de droits ou de responsabilités . Mais au XXe siècle, de plus en plus des Français choisissent une autre possibilité, le pacte civil de solidarité ou pacs, qui existe depuis 1999.

Janine Delacroix en est une: " On a le projet de nous pacser mon ami et moi. On attend de vivre
10 ensemble et de voir si ça marche. Je pense que l'on mettra chacun la même somme de côté tous les mois, sur un compte commun pour les achats communs comme les courses et le loyer et aussi un peu pour les vacances. Ensuite, chacun dépensera le reste comme il veut."

Le pacs avait pour but à l'origine de permettre aux couples homosexuels d'avoir les mêmes droits et obligations que les autres couples. Mais, depuis l'entrée en vigueur du pacs, ce sont surtout ces
15 couples de sexe différent qui décident de se pacser. Ainsi, en 2010 les pacs conclus entre homosexuels ne représentaient que 4,5% sur un total de 205.500 pacs. Le succès du pacs est tel que le nombre de pacs conclus n'est pas loin du nombre de mariages qui étaient de 245.300 en cette même année 2010.

La simplicité du pacs, et son caractère non traditionnel, alternatif, sont les explications les plus
20 souvent données pour expliquer le grand nombre enregistré. Se pacser est plus simple que se marier — et de même pour se dépacser que de divorcer — le pacs reste plus léger et les obligations sont moindres entre pacsés qu'entre personnes mariées. Ceci vaut au sujet du mariage civil; la différence est encore plus grande dans la comparaison entre pacs et mariage religieux.

Valérie Marchand a remarqué le nouveau vocabulaire qui arrive. "Se marier devient se pacser,
25 divorcer est devenu dépacser, un marié est un pacsé. Certains, encore peu nombreux, vont même jusqu'à circuler des listes de pacs, des listes de cadeaux pour fêter leur pacs. Par ailleurs, une cérémonie de pacs est aujourd'hui possible dans certaines mairies." *La différence entre mariage et pacs devient de moins en moins avec le temps, mais il reste cependant bien des différences entre les deux institutions. Par exemple, dans un mariage l'époux comme l'épouse a le droit d'usage du*
30 *nom de l'autre. Rien de tel pour les pacsés:* le pacs ne donne aucun droit d'employer le nom de l'autre partenaire. C'est pour cette raison que Valérie n'aime pas les pacs: "Lorsqu'une femme se pacse elle doit se faire toujours appeler Mademoiselle, et ne devient en aucun cas Madame. Elle ne porte pas le nom de son partenaire pacsé. Cela me déplait."

Dans un mariage, les époux bénéficient de la protection du logement familial: même si le mari est
35 seul propriétaire de leur maison, il doit demander à sa femme le droit de le vendre. Ce n'est pas le cas pour les pacsés. Si un couple marié a un enfant, le mari de la mère de l'enfant est présumé être le père. Pour l'enfant de parents pacsés, le père doit reconnaître l'enfant, sinon il n'a pas de droits. Seul le mariage permet l'adoption commune, les partenaires de pacs ne peuvent pas adopter ensemble. À la différence du mariage, mettre fin au pacs est assez simple, et peut être
40 fait par un seul des pacsés sans le consentement de l'autre, par déclaration faite au greffe du tribunal d'instance. Mettre fin au mariage nécessite l'une des procédures de divorce.

*les bans: 'banns' are published before a wedding can take place

MARKS

Questions

Re-read lines 1–8

1. The opening of the article discusses marriage in France.

    (a) You must meet three conditions to get married in France. State any **two** of them.   2

    (b) What changed in 2013?   1

    (c) In what way are marriages organised in France?   State **three** things.   3

Re-read lines 9–12

2. Janine talks about her plans to have a civil partnership with her boyfriend. What kind of things will their joint account be spent on? Mention **two** things for the mark.   1

Re-read lines 13–18

3. (a) What was the original intention for civil partnerships?   1

    (b) What has been the actual result? Give details.   3

Re-read lines 19–23

4. The writer gives several reasons for the popularity of civil partnerships. State any **two** details.   2

Re-read lines 24–33

5. The writer goes on to discuss the implications of civil partnerships.

    (a) According to Valérie, what is now possible?   1

    (b) Why does she not like civil partnerships?   1

Re-read lines 34–41

6. We learn of some differences between marriages and civil partnerships.

    (a) What can partners in a civil partnership not do?   1

    (b) What are the differences in the way relationships come to an end?   2

7. Now consider the article as a whole.

    Does the author give the impression that she is against civil partnerships? Give details from the text to justify your answer.   2

8. Translate into English:

    "La difference ... les pacsés." (*lines 27–30*)   **10**

[END OF MODEL QUESTION PAPER]

National
Qualifications
MODEL PAPER 2

French
Directed Writing

Duration — 1 hour and 40 minutes

Fill in these boxes and read what is printed below.

Full name of centre

Town

Forename(s)

Surname

Number of seat

Date of birth
Day   Month   Year

Scottish candidate number

Total marks — 10

Choose ONE scenario on *Page two* and write your answer clearly, in **French**, in the space provided in this booklet. You must clearly identify the scenario number you are attempting.

You may use a French dictionary.

Use **blue** or **black** ink.

There is a separate answer booklet for Reading. You must complete your answers for Reading in the answer booklet for Reading.

Before leaving the examination room you must give this Directed Writing question and answer booklet and your Reading answer booklet to the Invigilator; if you do not, you may lose all the marks for this paper.

Total marks — 10

Choose **one** of the following two scenarios.

SCENARIO 1: Learning

> You have recently returned from France, where you stayed with a French family to improve your French.
>
> On your return, you have been asked to write an account of your experiences to try to encourage other pupils to do the same thing.

You must include the following information and **you should try to add** other relevant details:

- Why you knew the family, **and** what the journey to their house was like

- What you did to improve your French

- How you got on with the family you stayed with

- If you would recommend such an experience to others

You should write approximately 120–150 words.

OR

SCENARIO 2: Employability

> Last summer you went to work in a colonie de vacances for young French children.
>
> On your return, you were asked to write a report, **in French**, of your experience.

You must include the following information and **you should try to add** other relevant details:

- What you thought of the accommodation **and** of your fellow workers
- What your duties were
- How you got on with the young children you were working with
- Whether you plan to repeat the exercise

You should write approximately 120–150 words.

ANSWER SPACE

MARKS | DO NOT WRITE IN THIS MARGIN

Scenario number

_____

_____

_____

_____

_____

_____

_____

_____

_____

_____

_____

_____

_____

_____

_____

_____

_____

_____

_____

_____

_____

_____

_____

_____

_____

_____

_____

ANSWER SPACE (continued)

MARKS

ANSWER SPACE (continued)

MARKS | DO NOT WRITE IN THIS MARGIN

ANSWER SPACE (continued)

[END OF MODEL QUESTION PAPER]

ADDITIONAL SPACE FOR ANSWERS

ADDITIONAL SPACE FOR ANSWERS

MARKS | DO NOT WRITE IN THIS MARGIN

National Qualifications
MODEL PAPER 2

French
Listening and Writing

Duration — 1 hour

Fill in these boxes and read what is printed below.

Full name of centre

Town

Forename(s)

Surname

Number of seat

Date of birth
Day   Month   Year

Scottish candidate number

Total marks — 30

SECTION 1 — LISTENING — 20 marks

You will hear two items in French. **Before you hear each item, you will have one minute to study the questions.** You will hear each item twice, with an interval of one minute between playings. You will then have time to answer the questions before hearing the next item. Write your answers clearly, in **English**, in the spaces provided.

SECTION 2 — WRITING — 10 marks

Write your answer clearly, in **French**, in the space provided.

Attempt ALL questions. You may use a French dictionary.

Additional space for answers is provided at the end of this booklet. If you use this space, you must clearly identify the question number you are attempting.

You are not allowed to leave the examination room until the end of the test.

Use **blue** or **black** ink.

Before leaving the examination room you must give your answer booklet to the Invigilator; if you do not, you may lose all the marks for this paper.

MARKS DO NOT WRITE IN THIS MARGIN

SECTION 1 — LISTENING — 20 marks
Attempt ALL questions

Item 1

You listen to a French teacher explaining what the 14th of July means in France.

(a) When exactly did the French people storm the Bastille?   1

_____

(b) What exactly do French people celebrate on 14th of July?   1

_____

(c) When was Louis XVI guillotined?   1

_____

(d) The speaker talks about what happens in France now on that day.

    (i) What does happen? State any **two** things.   2

    _____

    _____

    (ii) Where else do people celebrate July 14th?   1

    _____

(e) People discussed postponing the celebrations in 2014. Why was this?   1

_____

_____

(f) Overall, which statement best describes the speaker's opinion about July 14th? Tick (✓) the correct statement.   1

He says it is overdone in France	
He is very proud of the way it is celebrated	
He gives an explanation of where it comes from and what it is like now	

MARKS | DO NOT WRITE IN THIS MARGIN

Item 2

Mme Vernier describes the Parisian system of bike sharing, Vélib'.

(a) When exactly is the system available?   1

_____

(b) She talks about the costs to the users.

    (i) What is the cost for a daily membership?   1

    _____

    (ii) What is the advantage of an annual membership?   1

    _____

(c) Where can you find the bicycles?   1

_____

(d) She talks about the 'bornes', or interfaces.

    (i) What does a borne allow you to do?   1

    _____

    (ii) What is the other advantage of having an annual membership?   1

    _____

    _____

(e) She says the bikes have several features. State any **two** features.   2

_____

(f) Who can get a membership for 19€ instead of 39€?   1

_____

(g) She refers to several methods you can use to pay for the service. State any **one**.   1

_____

(h) What do people between 14 and 18 need to have to be able to use the bikes?   1

_____

MARKS | DO NOT WRITE IN THIS MARGIN

SECTION 2 — WRITING — 10 marks

Mme Vernier nous a parlé de 'Vélib'.

Est-ce-que tu fais du vélo? Quand?

C'est une bonne chose pour ta santé?

Penses-tu que c'est une bonne idée pour l'environnement?

Ecris 120—150 mots en français pour exprimer tes idées.

_____

_____

_____

_____

_____

_____

_____

_____

_____

_____

_____

_____

_____

_____

_____

_____

_____

MARKS | DO NOT WRITE IN THIS MARGIN

ANSWER SPACE FOR SECTION 2 (continued)

[END OF MODEL QUESTION PAPER]

ADDITIONAL SPACE FOR ANSWERS

MARKS

DO NOT
WRITE IN
THIS
MARGIN

ADDITIONAL SPACE FOR ANSWERS

National
Qualifications
MODEL PAPER 2

French
Listening Transcript

Duration — 1 hour

This paper must not be seen by any candidate.

The material overleaf is provided for use in an emergency only (eg the recording or equipment proving faulty) or where permission has been given in advance by SQA for the material to be read to candidates with additional support needs. The material must be read exactly as printed.

HODDER
GIBSON
LEARN MORE

Transcript — Higher

> **Instructions to reader(s):**
>
> For each item, read the English **once**, then read the French **twice**, with an interval of 1 minute between the two readings. On completion of the second reading, pause for the length of time indicated in brackets after the item, to allow the candidates to write their answers.
>
> Where special arrangements have been agreed in advance to allow the reading of the material, those sections marked **(f)** should be read by a female speaker and those marked **(m)** by a male; those sections marked **(t)** should be read by the teacher.

(t)   **Item 1**

You listen to a French teacher explaining what the 14th of July means in France.

You now have one minute to study the questions for Item 1.

(m/f) Le matin du 14 juillet 1789, le peuple de Paris prend des armes aux Invalides puis marche vers une forteresse royale, la Bastille. Après une courte bataille, il libère les prisonniers qui y étaient enfermés. La prise de la Bastille est une première victoire du peuple de Paris contre un symbole de l'Ancien Régime.

Le 14 juillet 1789, alors, c'est ce qu'on célèbre à la fête nationale? Ce n'est vraiment pas le cas. Les Anglais parlent du « Bastille Day » , mais c'est la Fête de la Fédération qui est commémoré chaque 14 juillet. Elle marque la fin de la monarchie absolue, célébrée pour la première fois en 1790 au Champ-de-Mars de Paris. Louis XVI a assisté à cette fête, avant d'être guillotiné trois ans plus tard.

C'est un jour férié, et partout en France il y a des bals, et des feux d'artifice dans la nuit du 14 au 15 Juillet. Il y a aussi un défilé des troupes sur les Champs-Élysées, et des défilés ou des cérémonies militaires dans la plupart des villes de la France et aussi dans les territoires et les départements outre-mer, comme Tahiti et Martinique.

En 2014 le journal Le Figaro a affirmé que le défilé pourrait être repoussé au lendemain si l'équipe de France atteignait la finale de la Coupe du monde, le président de la République François Hollande a n'a pas accepté cette idée.

(2 minutes)

(t) Item 2

Mme Vernier describes the Parisian system of bike sharing, Vélib'.

You now have one minute to study the questions for Item 2.

(m) **C'est quoi, Vélib'?**

(f) C'est un système où on peut prendre un vélo dans une station, le déposer dans une autre, Vélib' est un système de location de vélos, disponible 24 heures sur 24 et 7 jours sur 7.

(m) **Et ça coûte combien?**

(f) On peut payer 1.70€ par jour, 8€ par semaine, ou le meilleur, 39€ par an pour un abonnement avec un nombre de trajets illimités et les 45 premières minutes gratuites pour chacun de vos voyages.

(m) **Il est facile de trouver des stations Vélib' à Paris?**

(f) Il y a beaucoup de stations disponibles dans Paris, distantes de 300 mètres environ. Elles sont constituées d'une borne et de points d'attache pour les vélos. Chaque station est équipée de jusqu'à 70 vélos.

(m) **Qu'est-ce que c'est une borne?**

(f) C'est une terminale, une sorte d'ordinateur qui contrôle l'accès aux vélos. La borne Vélib' vous permet de louer un vélo. Identifiez-vous sur la borne, accédez au menu et choisissez un vélo parmi ceux proposés à l'écran. Vous pouvez gagner du temps si vous vous abonnez à l'année. Grâce à une carte annuelle Vélib' vous pouvez retirer un vélo directement sur le point d'attache, sans passer par la borne.

(m) **Comment sont les vélos?**

(f) Un Vélib', c'est un vélo mixte pour homme ou femme - une selle qu'on peut ajuster et un panier de grande capacité. En plus, les feux éclairent tout au long du trajet.

(m) **Comment est-ce qu'on retourne son vélo?**

(f) Une fois votre trajet terminé, accrochez le vélo sur un point d'attache libre dans n'importe quelle station Vélib'. Attendez quelques instants, un signal sonore et une petite lumière vous confirmeront que le vélo a bien été restitué.

(m) **Est-ce qu'il y a des tarifs différents pour les étudiants?**

(f) Oui, si vous avez entre 14 et 26 ans et faîtes des études, la formule Vélib' Passion vous permet de profiter des avantages de l'abonnement pour seulement 19€/ par an au lieu de 39€/ par an. On peut payer par carte bancaire, par chèques bancaires ou par une souscription en ligne.

(m) **Quel est l'âge minimum requis pour souscrire un abonnement?**

(f) Pour des raisons de sécurité, en particulier la taille des vélos, le service est accessible à partir de 14 ans. Pour les personnes âgées entre 14 et 18 ans, l'autorisation du parent ou responsable légal est obligatoire.

(m) **Merci pour les informations.**

(f) Bon voyage !

(2 minutes)

(t) **End of test.**

Now look over your answers.

[END OF MODEL TRANSCRIPT]

HIGHER FOR CfE FRENCH 2014   84   HODDER GIBSON MODEL PAPERS

Model Paper 3

Whilst this Model Practice Paper has been specially commissioned by Hodder Gibson for use as practice for the Higher (for Curriculum for Excellence) exams, the key reference document remains the SQA Specimen Paper 2014.

HODDER
GIBSON
LEARN MORE

National Qualifications
MODEL PAPER 3

French
Reading

Duration — 1 hour and 40 minutes

Total marks — 30

Attempt ALL questions.

Write your answers clearly, in **English**, in the Reading answer booklet. In the answer booklet you must clearly identify the question number you are attempting.

You may use a French dictionary.

Use **blue** or **black** ink.

There is a separate question and answer booklet for Directed Writing. You must complete your answer for Directed Writing in the question and answer booklet for Directed Writing.

Before leaving the examination room you must give your Reading answer booklet and your Directed Writing question and answer booklet to the Invigilator; if you do not, you may lose all the marks for this paper.

Total marks — 30

Attempt ALL questions

Read the whole article carefully and then answer, in English, ALL the questions that follow.

In this article, the writer gives advice on preparing for a job interview .

Comment préparer un entretien d'embauche

Vous devez réserver au moins une demi-journée pour vous préparer. L'idéal est de commencer dès que vous avez votre rendez-vous. D'abord: organiser toutes les détailles sur l'entreprise, et l'annonce à laquelle vous répondez. Alice, par exemple, raconte: " Ayant répondu à plusieurs annonces, je ne savais finalement plus pour quel poste exactement je
5   postulais lorsque je suis arrivée à l'entretien pour la poste. Bien sûr, je ne l'ai pas eu. "

Vous devez absolument vous renseigner sur l'entreprise pour laquelle vous postulez. Visitez son site internet, préparez-vous bien et rassemblez un maximum d'informations sur l'entreprise. Cette recherche prouvera votre motivation.

Si vous avez des amis à vous qui ont déjà fait un stage chez l'entreprise, vous pouvez aussi les
10   appeler pour leur demander des renseignements. Pourquoi ces recherches ? Pour être plus informé, plus réactif en entretien et prouver ainsi votre motivation, voire votre connaissance du secteur et du métier. Jean nous raconte son histoire. " J'ai eu un entretien que j'ai totalement raté, jusqu'au point que le recruteur m'a dit que c'était presque catastrophique et qu'il me donne la réponse tout de suite, que c'était non. Il a dit que, si je voulais toujours
15   postuler pour une autre fois, il me fallait m'avoir bien préparé."

Analysez les expériences que vous avez mentionnées sur votre CV. Qu'est-ce que vous avez appris de ces expériences qui pourraient l'intéresser ? Quelles "activités extra-professionnelle" professionelles avez-vous indiqué ? Démontrent-elles que vous avez les qualités requises pour le poste ? Pourquoi ? Demandez-vous quelles sont vos faiblesses pour le poste : le recruteur les
20   aura probablement vues lui aussi. Il va à un certain point concentrer là-dessus. Des périodes de chômage, un changement d'orientation, une manque d'expériences satisfaisantes.

Réfléchissez à ce que vous répondriez à une douzaine de questions classiques d'un entretien d'embauche, tels : Préférez-vous travailler seul ou en équipe ? Qu'est-ce qui vous motive dans la vie ? Quelles sont vos qualités ? Et vos défauts ? Pourquoi postulez-vous pour ce poste ?
25   Si nous vous offrons ce poste, que feriez-vous? Comment vous voyez-vous dans dix ans ? Nous avons déjà reçu de nombreux candidats, pourquoi devrais-je vous retenir ? Même si on ne vous pose pas ces questions-là exactement, cela vous apprendra à parler de vous-même et à savoir vous "vendre". *Rafraîchissez-vous la mémoire avec des informations sur votre employeur actuel. On attend de vous que vous en sachiez beaucoup sur l'entreprise pour*
30   *laquelle vous travaillez. Préparez les questions que vous voulez vous-même poser. N'oubliez pas qu'un entretien est aussi un échange.*

Le jour de l'entretien, soyez à l'heure. Rien n'est plus pénible qu'un candidat qui doit se justifier parce qu'il est en retard. Renseignez-vous précisément sur l'endroit où se trouve l'entreprise, sur les transports en commun à prendre ou sur les possibilités de parking. Tenez
35   compte du fait que vous pouvez vous retrouver dans les bouchons ou que votre train peut avoir du retard. Présentez-vous une dizaine de minutes avant l'heure convenue. Vous devrez peut-être encore compléter quelques formulaires avant le début de l'entretien. Vous devez savoir où et quand a lieu l'entretien, à connaître le nom de l'intervieweur et à savoir son rôle dans l'entreprise.

40   Soyez attentif à votre habillement, que vous adapterez de préférence à la culture de l'organisation et au travail pour lequel vous postulez. Si vous ne devrez jamais mettre de costume dans la fonction en question, il n'est pas nécessaire d'en mettre un pour l'entretien. Prenez avec vous votre lettre de convocation, plusieurs CV, car vous aurez peut-être à le donner à plusieurs personnes qui ne l'ont pas eu, et l'original ou une copie de vos diplômes.
45   Un conseil : mettez tout cela dans un trieur pour ne pas donner l'impression d'être en fouillis.

MARKS

Questions

Re-read lines 1–5

1. The opening of the article discusses the initial steps to make. What did Alice do wrong? State **two** details.   2

Re-read lines 6–15

2. The article then goes on to tell you what to do next.

   (a) In what way might your friends be of use to you? State **two** details.   2

   (b) What are the advantages of doing thorough research?   2

   (c) What was Jean told?   1

Re-read lines 16–21

3. The writer discusses three important things should you consider before the interview.

   (a) Why should you think about your weaknesses?   1

   (b) What examples of potential weaknesses does the writer give? Give any **two** examples.   2

Re-read lines 22–31

4. The writer gives examples of questions an interviewer might ask you. Why should you think about these questions?   1

Re-read lines 32–39

5. The writer discusses the day of the interview.

   (a) In what way can you avoid being late?   1

   (b) When should you arrive? Why?   1

MARKS

Re-read lines 40–45

6. The writer gives further advice on the day of the interview.

    (a) What does he say about how you should dress? State any **two** details.   2

    (b) State any **two** things you should bring with you.   2

    (c) What is his final piece of advice?   1

7. Now consider the article as a whole.

    Does the writer give the impression that a job interview is straightforward? Give details from the text to justify your answer.   2

8. Translate into English:

    " Rafraîchissez-vous ... échange" (*lines 28-31*)   10

[END OF MODEL QUESTION PAPER]

National
Qualifications
MODEL PAPER 3

French
Directed Writing

Duration — 1 hour and 40 minutes

Fill in these boxes and read what is printed below.

Full name of centre

Town

Forename(s)

Surname

Number of seat

Date of birth
Day   Month   Year

Scottish candidate number

Total marks — 10

Choose ONE scenario on *Page two* and write your answer clearly, in **French**, in the space provided in this booklet. You must clearly identify the scenario number you are attempting.

You may use a French dictionary.

Use **blue** or **black** ink.

There is a separate answer booklet for Reading. You must complete your answers for Reading in the answer booklet for Reading.

Before leaving the examination room you must give this Directed Writing question and answer booklet and your Reading answer booklet to the Invigilator; if you do not, you may lose all the marks for this paper.

Total marks — 10

Choose **one** of the following two scenarios.

SCENARIO 1: Learning

> You have recently returned from France, where you have spent two weeks attending a French school.
>
> On your return, you have been asked to write an account of your experiences to try to encourage other pupils to do the same thing.

You must include the following information and **you should try to add** other relevant details:

- Where the school was, **and** how you got there
- What you did while you were at the school
- How you got on with the other pupils and the teachers
- If you would recommend such an experience to others

You should write approximately 120–150 words.

OR

SCENARIO 2: Culture

> Last year you went with a French friend to a holiday camp in the South of France. While you were there you took part in many activities.
>
> On your return you were asked to write a report, **in French**, of your visit.

You must include the following information and **you should try to add** other relevant details:

- Where exactly the camp was **and** what you thought of the accommodation
- What you did during the day
- How you got on with the other young people there
- How you plan to develop the links you made there

You should write approximately 120–150 words.

ANSWER SPACE

Scenario number

ANSWER SPACE (continued)

ANSWER SPACE (continued)

ANSWER SPACE (continued)

[END OF MODEL QUESTION PAPER]

MARKS

DO NOT WRITE IN THIS MARGIN

ADDITIONAL SPACE FOR ANSWERS

MARKS DO NOT WRITE IN THIS MARGIN

ADDITIONAL SPACE FOR ANSWERS

National
Qualifications
MODEL PAPER 3

French
Listening and Writing

Duration — 1 hour

Fill in these boxes and read what is printed below.

Full name of centre

Town

Forename(s)

Surname

Number of seat

Date of birth
Day   Month   Year

Scottish candidate number

Total marks — 30

SECTION 1 — LISTENING — 20 marks

You will hear two items in French. **Before you hear each item, you will have one minute to study the questions.** You will hear each item twice, with an interval of one minute between playings. You will then have time to answer the questions before hearing the next item. Write your answers clearly, in **English**, in the spaces provided.

SECTION 2 — WRITING — 10 marks

Write your answer clearly, in **French**, in the space provided.

Attempt ALL questions. You may use a French dictionary.

Additional space for answers is provided at the end of this booklet. If you use this space, you must clearly identify the question number you are attempting.

You are not allowed to leave the examination room until the end of the test.

Use **blue** or **black** ink.

Before leaving the examination room you must give your answer booklet to the Invigilator; if you do not, you may lose all the marks for this paper.

HODDER GIBSON
LEARN MORE

MARKS | DO NOT WRITE IN THIS MARGIN

SECTION 1 — LISTENING — 20 marks
Attempt ALL questions

Item 1

You listen to a French government official describing 'Francophonie'.

(a) In what way does he define Francophonie?   **1**

_____

(b) How many people are estimated to speak French across the world?   **1**

_____

(c) What does he say is important to the French government? State **two** things.   **2**

_____

_____

(d) The speaker talks about the importance of developments in the digital world.

  (i) What does France want to do?   **1**

_____

  (ii) What steps will France take in order to do this?   **1**

_____

(e) What is the aim of the Francophone innovation network launched in 2013?   **2**

_____

_____

(f) Overall, which statement best describes the speaker's opinion about Francophonie? Tick (✓) the correct statement.   **1**

He says France has fallen far behind English	
He is very proud of the way French is the language of diplomacy	
He thinks French has to work hard to maintain its role in the world	

MARKS | DO NOT WRITE IN THIS MARGIN

Item 2

Anjela discusses the situation of Breton, the language spoken in Brittany.

(a) How many people currently can speak Breton?   **1**

_____

(b) Anjela compares Breton to Scots Gaelic.

  (i) What does she say about the number of speakers of each language?   **1**

  _____

  (ii) She talks about a difference between the two languages. What is it?   **1**

  _____

(c) What has Unesco said about Breton?   **1**

_____

(d) Anjela discusses the recent changes in the situation of Breton.

  (i) What has changed since the last century?   **1**

  _____

  (ii) She talks about some particular changes. State any **two** of them.   **2**

  _____

  _____

(e) Anjela talks about changes in the number of young people speaking Breton. Give **two** details.   **2**

_____

_____

(f) How long is Breton broadcast on the radio for?   **1**

_____

(g) What is the main variation between the different dialects of Breton?   **1**

_____

SECTION 2 — WRITING — 10 marks

Anjela nous a parlé du Breton.

Est-ce-que tu parles ou Gaélique ou Scots? Pourquoi ou pourquoi pas?

Est-ce-que tu crois que parler au moins une seconde langue est importante?

Penses-tu que parler une autre langue peut aider dans une future carrière?

Ecris 120—150 mots en français pour exprimer tes idées

MARKS | DO NOT WRITE IN THIS MARGIN

ANSWER SPACE FOR SECTION 2 (continued)

[END OF MODEL QUESTION PAPER]

ADDITIONAL SPACE FOR ANSWERS

MARKS

DO NOT WRITE IN THIS MARGIN

ADDITIONAL SPACE FOR ANSWERS

National Qualifications
MODEL PAPER 3

French
Listening Transcript

Duration — 1 hour

This paper must not be seen by any candidate.

The material overleaf is provided for use in an emergency only (eg the recording or equipment proving faulty) or where permission has been given in advance by SQA for the material to be read to candidates with additional support needs. The material must be read exactly as printed.

Transcript — Higher

> **Instructions to reader(s):**
>
> For each item, read the English **once**, then read the French **twice**, with an interval of 1 minute between the two readings. On completion of the second reading, pause for the length of time indicated in brackets after the item, to allow the candidates to write their answers.
>
> Where special arrangements have been agreed in advance to allow the reading of the material, those sections marked **(f)** should be read by a female speaker and those marked **(m)** by a male; those sections marked **(t)** should be read by the teacher.

(t)   **Item 1**

You listen to a French government official describing 'Francophonie'.

You now have one minute to study the questions for Item 1.

(m/f) La francophonie est le mot qui décrit tous les pays et toutes les personnes qui parlent le français. La francophonie, ce sont nous, tout d'abord des femmes et des hommes qui partagent une langue commune, le français. Le dernier rapport de l'Observatoire de la langue française, publié en 2010, estime leur nombre à 220 millions de locuteurs répartis sur les cinq continents. Le français cohabite dans de nombreux pays francophones avec des langues nationales ou transnationales africaines, les créoles, l'arabe, et les langues européennes.

Soutenir et développer l'enseignement et l'usage de la langue française dans le monde ainsi que dans la vie diplomatique et internationale est d'une grande importance à nous tous, et au gouvernement français.

La participation des francophones de tous âges, professions, intérêts et talents au domaine digitale est maintenant une priorité pour la France. Elle veut défendre la diversité culturelle sur internet, par exemple en soutenant la production de contenus en français, et en mettant des textes littéraires en ligne. Créé en 2013, le réseau francophone de l'innovation a lancé une plateforme collaborative, qui offre à la communauté francophone des ressources en français. Nous voulons que le Français reste un joueur important dans le monde du XXIème siècle

(2 minutes)

(t)   **Item 2**

Anjela discusses the situation of Breton, the language spoken in Brittany.

You now have one minute to study the questions for Item 2.

(m) **Bonjour Anjela, tu es bretonnante, alors tu parles le breton. Est-ce que tu peux nous raconter un peu de la langue bretonne en France?**

(f)   Bonjour Yannik, bien sûr. Le breton est une langue celtique parlée par 200 000 personnes en Bretagne. Elle appartient au groupe des langues celtiques, c'est-à-dire originaires de la Grande Bretagne. Mais comme en Ecosse, sa pratique traditionnelle est concentrée dans l'ouest du pays.

(m) **Alors la situation est comme le Gaélique en Ecosse?**

(f)   Nous avons plus de deux fois plus de parleurs que du Gaélique en Ecosse. Le Gaélique est langue officielle de l'Ecosse, tandis que le breton est reconnu comme langue régional ou minoritaire de France. Il est classé comme « langue sérieusement en danger » par UNESCO.

(m) **Est-ce que la situation du breton a changé récemment, comme celle du Gaélique après la création du parlement écossais?**

(f)   La langue bretonne, qui avait décliné au XXe siècle, connaît depuis les années 2000 un certain regain. Les écoles associatives Diwan, qui donnent des cours en breton, y ont aidé. Elles sont quarante et une et ont à peu près 4000 élèves. Grâce aux subventions, les éditeurs publient plus de livres en breton que jamais. Et sur les panneaux routiers, on trouve, en général, le nom des villes et villages en français et en breton, à la suite de la campagne de l'Office de la langue bretonne.

(m) **Est-ce que beaucoup de jeunes parlent le breton?**

(f)   À la fin du XXe siècle il y avait très précisément moins de 500 jeunes de 15 à 19 ans capables de parler breton. Aujourd'hui, la part des jeunes de 15-19 capables de s'exprimer en breton est passée à plusieurs milliers. Mais n'oublions pas que des 200 000 locuteurs du breton, 60 % sont retraités.

(m) **Est-ce que la radio et la télé soutiennent le breton?**

(f)   Bien sûr, les médias jouent un rôle important dans la diffusion de la langue bretonne. Mais il s'agit des émissions de radio et de télévision en breton, car il n'y a toujours pas de chaînes de télévision émettant en breton, comme Alba en gaélique en Écosse par exemple. En ce qui concerne la radio, les stations locales diffusent plusieurs heures d'émissions en breton par semaine, c'est tout.

(m) **Est-ce que le breton varie d'un endroit à l'autre de la Bretagne?**

(f)   Bien sûr, comme la majorité des langues, la langue bretonne varie d'un endroit à l'autre. En breton, ces différences entre les dialectes touchent avant tout la prononciation et une petite partie du vocabulaire.

(m) **Merci pour les informations.**

(f)   Je vous en prie.

(2 minutes)

(t)   **End of test.**

Now look over your answers.

[END OF MODEL TRANSCRIPT]

HIGHER FOR CfE | ANSWER SECTION

SQA AND HODDER GIBSON HIGHER FOR CfE FRENCH 2014

Reading

Question		Expected Answer(s)
1.		• A lot of people are leaving towns in summer • A lot of people go to escape daily life • Go away not just in summer, but also in winter • People are still taking short breaks *Any 2 points from possible 4 for 2 marks*
2.	(a)	• To escape from work • Many people have to work extra hours and are exhausted • They still have to look after children when go home
	(b)	• You risk ending up doing household tasks
3.	(a)	• They stay closer to home
	(b)	• There is always something to discover close by • They can visit factories, nuclear power stations or cheese factories *Any 1 point from possible 2 for 1 mark*
4.	(a)	• People can do a variety of sports during the day • They have opportunity to get together in the evening with friends and family OR get together in the evening to chat / sing / have a drink
	(b)	• People get benefit of fresh air whether they do physical activity or not • Wake up to lovely views
5.	(a)	• They return from holiday with a tan
	(b)	• They spend hours stuck in the car because of traffic jams • There are so many people on beach it is difficult to find space to lie down on the sand
6.		• It's less expensive • Opportunity to be closer to nature • Think about animals/beauty of surroundings

Question		Expected Answer(s)
7.		Outline of possible response and evidence: • The writer gives the impression that holidays are a necessity. **Possible evidence includes:** • Writer states French people have no intention of giving up holidays (despite rise in cost of living) • Writer states large numbers of French people continue to go on summer and winter holidays and short breaks • Writer states it is necessary to get away from office to rest/escape daily routine/do what you like • Economic crisis has meant people staying closer to home, but not giving up holidays entirely • Examples such as in the mountains it is a chance to be with family: mountain air will do you good - implies necessary to get away; getting a tan implies relaxation is necessary; • Choosing to stay in cabins rather than hotels implies people not prepared to give up holidays, but will find cheaper ways of going away; types of activities (eg walking/fishing) imply don't need to spend much money to go away
8.		**Translation** Cependant, l'année dernière, beaucoup de Français ont choisi **However, last year a lot of French people chose** de passer leurs vacances à la campagne qui a tant de choses à offrir. **to spend their holidays in the country which has so much/so many things to offer** Par exemple, on peut passer des journées au bord d'une rivière à pêcher **For example, you can spend days on the banks of a river fishing** ou même faire une promenade en vélo en forêt **or even go for a bike ride in the forest** tout en découvrant l'histoire de la région **while finding out about the history of the area**

Directed Writing

Candidates will write a piece of extended writing in French addressing a scenario that has four related bullet points. Candidates must address each bullet point. The first bullet point contains two pieces of information to be addressed. The remaining three bullet points contain one piece of information each. There is a choice of two scenarios and learners must choose one of these.

Mark	Content	Accuracy	Language resource: variety, range, structures
10	• The content is comprehensive • All bullet points are addressed fully and some candidates may also provide additional relevant information	• The language is accurate in all four bullets However, where the candidate attempts to go beyond the range of the task, a slightly higher number of inaccuracies need not detract from the overall very good impression • A comprehensive range of verbs is used accurately and tenses are consistent and accurate • There is evidence of confident handling of all aspects of grammar and accurate spelling, although the language may contain a number of minor errors, or even one serious error • Where the candidate attempts to go beyond the range of the task, a slightly higher number of inaccuracies need not detract from the overall very good impression	• The language used is detailed and complex • There is good use of adjectives, adverbs, prepositional phrases and, where appropriate, word order • A comprehensive range of verbs/verb forms, tenses and constructions is used • Some modal verbs and infinitives may be used • The candidate is comfortable with the first person of the verb and generally uses a different verb in each sentence • Sentences are mainly complex and accurate • The language flows well
8	• The content is clear • All bullet points are addressed clearly. The response to one bullet point may be thin, although other bullet points are dealt with in some detail	• The language is mostly accurate. Where the candidate attempts to use detailed and complex language, this may be less successful, although basic structures are used accurately • A range of verbs is used accurately and tenses are generally consistent and accurate • There may be a few errors in spelling, adjective endings and, where relevant, case endings. Use of accents is less secure, where relevant	• The language used is detailed and complex • In one bullet point the language may be more basic than might otherwise be expected at this level • The candidate uses a range of verbs/verb forms and other constructions • There may be less variety in the verbs used • The candidate is comfortable with the first person of the verb and generally uses a different verb in each sentence • Sentences are generally complex and mainly accurate • Overall the writing will be very competent, essentially correct, but may be pedestrian

Mark	Content	Accuracy	Language resource: variety, range, structures
6	• The content is adequate and may be similar to that of an 8 • Bullet points may be addressed adequately, however one of the bullet points may not be addressed	• The language may be mostly accurate in two or three bullet points. However, in the remaining one or two, control of the language structure may deteriorate significantly • The verbs are generally correct, but basic • Tenses may be inconsistent, with present tenses being used at times instead of past tenses • There may be errors in spelling, adjective endings and some prepositions may be inaccurate or omitted. There are quite a few errors in other parts of speech – personal pronouns, gender of nouns, adjective endings, cases (where relevant), singular/plural confusion – and in the use of accents (where relevant) • Overall, there is more correct than incorrect and there is the impression that the candidate can handle tenses	• There are some examples of detailed and complex language • The language is perhaps repetitive and uses a limited range of verbs and fixed phrases not appropriate to this level • The candidate relies on a limited range of vocabulary and structures • There is minimal use of adjectives, probably mainly after "is" • The candidate has a limited knowledge of plurals • A limited range of verbs is used to address some of the bullet points • The candidate copes with the past tense of some verbs • When using the perfect tense, the past participle is incorrect or the auxiliary verb is omitted on occasion • Sentences are mainly single clause and may be brief
4	• The content may be limited and the Directed Writing may be presented as a single paragraph • Bullet points may be addressed in a limited way. or • **Two** of the bullet points are not be addressed	• The language is mainly inaccurate and after the first bullet the control of the language structure may deteriorate significantly. • A limited range of verbs is used • Ability to form tenses is inconsistent • In the use of the perfect tense the auxiliary verb is omitted on a number of occasions • There may be confusion between the singular and plural form of verbs • There are errors in many other parts of speech – gender of nouns, cases, singular/plural confusion – and in spelling and, where appropriate, word order • Several errors are serious, perhaps showing mother tongue interference	• There is limited use of detailed and complex language • The language is repetitive, with undue reliance on fixed phrases and a limited range of common basic verbs such as to be, to have, to play, to watch • The candidate mainly copes only with simple language • The verbs "was" and "went" may also be used correctly • Sentences are basic and there may be one sentence that is not intelligible to a sympathetic native speaker • An English word may appear in the writing or a word may be omitted • There may be an example of serious dictionary misuse
2	• The content may be basic or similar to that of a 4 or even a 6 • Bullet points are addressed with difficulty.	• The language is inaccurate in all four bullets and there is little control of language structure • Many of the verbs are incorrect or even omitted. There is little evidence of tense control • There are many errors in other parts of speech — personal pronouns, gender of nouns, cases, singular/plural confusion, prepositions, for instance	• There is little use, if any, of detailed and complex language • Verbs used more than once may be written differently on each occasion • The candidate displays almost no knowledge of the past tense of verbs • The candidate cannot cope with more than one or two basic verbs • Sentences are very short and some sentences may not be understood by a sympathetic native speaker

Mark	Content	Accuracy	Language resource: variety, range, structures
0	• The content is very basic. • The candidate is unable to address the bullet points Or • **Three** or more of the bullet points are not be addressed	• The language is seriously inaccurate in all four bullets and there is almost no control of language structure • Most errors are serious • Virtually nothing is correct • Very little is intelligible to a sympathetic native speaker	• There is no evidence of detailed and complex language • The candidate may only cope with the verbs to have and to be • There may be several examples of mother tongue interference. • English words are used • Very few words are written correctly in the modern language. • There may be several examples of serious dictionary misuse

Section 1 — Listening

Item 1

Question			Expected Answer(s)
1.	(a)		• The current system is not efficient
	(b)	(i)	• They can spend up to 40 hours a week
		(ii)	• French pupils do not have better results than their European neighbours/than Spanish, German and British pupils.
	(c)		• School day would be shorter • There would be a maximum of 7 hours of classes a day • Pupils would finish at 17.00/5pm *Any two of above 3 points for 2 marks*
	(d)		• Pupils would be able to concentrate / be more attentive in class • Pupils would be less tired in class • They would be able to do sport / extra curricular activities • They would have more time to relax *Any two of above 4 points for 2 marks*
	(e)		They will improve performance

Item 2

Question			Expected Answer(s)
2.	(a)		• She cannot do what she wants to do
	(b)	(i)	• She loves chatting in any language • Her languages teachers are all nice • Language lessons are always interesting *Any two of above 3 points for 2 marks*
		(ii)	• In that class you must only speak Spanish • You progress faster
	(c)	(i)	• Interpreter for the European Parliament in Strasbourg
		(ii)	• A lot of students at the university are bilingual
		(iii)	• Employers look for languages that are a bit different, such as Chinese
	(d)	(i)	• She has worked in a holiday camp for two summers/each summer she works in a holiday camp • She has been babysitting since the age of 14
		(ii)	• Both her parents are teachers and they love their job • Teachers have very long holidays.

Section 2 — Writing

Candidates will write 120–150 words in a piece of extended writing in French addressing a stimulus of three questions in French.

Mark	Content	Accuracy	Language resource: variety, range, structures
10	• The content is comprehensive • The topic is addressed fully, in a balanced way • Some candidates may also provide additional information. • Overall this comes over as a competent, well thought-out response to the task which reads naturally.	• The language is accurate throughout. However where the candidate attempts to go beyond the range of the task, a slightly higher number of inaccuracies need not detract from the overall very good impression • A comprehensive range of verbs is used accurately and tenses are consistent and accurate • There is evidence of confident handling of all aspects of grammar and spelling accurately, although the language may contain a number of minor errors, or even one serious major error	• The language used is detailed and complex • There is good use of adjectives, adverbs, prepositional phrases and, where appropriate, word order. • A comprehensive range of verbs/verb forms, tenses and constructions is used. • Some modal verbs and infinitives may be used. • The candidate is comfortable with the first person of the verb and generally uses a different verb in each sentence. • The candidate uses co-ordinating conjunctions and subordinate clauses throughout the writing. • Sentences are mainly complex and accurate. • The language flows well
8	• The content is clear • The topic is addressed clearly	• The language is mostly accurate. However where the candidate attempts to use detailed and complex language, this may be less successful, although basic structures are used accurately • A range of verbs is used accurately and tenses are generally consistent and accurate • There may be a few errors in spelling, adjective endings and, where relevant, case endings. Use of accents is less secure. • Verbs and other parts of speech are used accurately but simply.	The language used is detailed and complex • The candidate uses a range of verbs/verb forms and other constructions. • There may be less variety in the verbs used. • The candidate is comfortable with the first person of the verb and generally uses a different verb in each sentence. • Most of the more complex sentences use co-ordinating conjunctions, and there may also be examples of subordinating conjunctions where appropriate. • Sentences are generally complex and mainly accurate. • At times the language may be more basic than might otherwise be expected at this level. • There may be an example of minor misuse of dictionary. • Overall the writing will be very competent, essentially correct, but may be pedestrian.

Mark	Content	Accuracy	Language resource: variety, range, structures
6	• The content is adequate and may be similar to that of an 8 or a 10 • The topic is addressed adequately	• The language may be mostly accurate. However, in places, control of the language structure may deteriorate significantly. • The verbs are generally correct, but basic. Tenses may be inconsistent, with present tenses being used at times instead of past tenses. • There may be errors in spelling, e.g. reversal of vowel combinations adjective endings and some prepositions may be inaccurate or omitted, e.g. I went the town. There are quite a few errors in other parts of speech – personal pronouns, gender of nouns, adjective endings, cases, singular/plural confusion – and in the use of accents • Overall, there is more correct than incorrect and there is the impression that the candidate can handle tenses	• There are some examples of detailed and complex language • The language is perhaps repetitive and uses a limited range of verbs and fixed phrases not appropriate to this level. • The candidate relies on a limited range of vocabulary and structures. • There is minimal use of adjectives, probably mainly after "is". • The candidate has a limited knowledge of plurals. • The candidate copes with the present tense of most verbs. • Where the candidate attempts constructions with modal verbs, these are not always successful. • Sentences are mainly single clause and may be brief • There may be some misuse of dictionary
4	• The content may be limited and may be presented as a single paragraph • The topic is addressed in a limited way	• The language used to address the more predictable aspects of the task may be accurate. However, major errors occur when the candidate attempts to address a less predictable aspect. • A limited range of verbs is used. • Ability to form tenses is inconsistent. • In the use of the perfect tense the auxiliary verb is omitted on a number of occasions. • There may be confusion between the singular and plural form of verbs. • There are errors in many other parts of speech – gender of nouns, cases, singular/plural confusion – and in spelling and, where appropriate, word order. • Several errors are serious, perhaps showing mother tongue interference. • Overall there is more incorrect than correct.	• There is limited use of detailed and complex language and the language is mainly simple and predictable • The language is repetitive, with undue reliance on fixed phrases and a limited range of common basic verbs such as to be, to have, to play, to watch. • There is inconsistency in the use of various expressions, especially verbs. • Sentences are basic and there may be one sentence that is not intelligible to a sympathetic native speaker. • An English word may appear in the writing or a word may be omitted. • There may be an example of serious dictionary misuse.
2	• The content may be basic or similar to that of a 4 or even a 6 • The topic is thinly addressed	• The language is almost completely inaccurate throughout the writing and there is little control of language structure • Many of the verbs are incorrect or even omitted. There is little evidence of tense control. • There are many errors in other parts of speech — personal pronouns, gender of nouns, cases, singular/plural confusion • Prepositions are not used correctly.	• There is little use, if any, of detailed and complex language • The candidate has a very limited vocabulary. • Verbs used more than once may be written differently on each occasion. • The candidate cannot cope with more than one or two basic verbs. • Sentences are very short and some sentences may not be understood by a sympathetic native speaker • Several English or "made-up" words may appear in the writing. • There are examples of serious dictionary misuse.

Mark	Content	Accuracy	Language resource: variety, range, structures
0	• The content is very basic. • The candidate is unable to address the topic.	• The language is seriously inaccurate throughout the writing and there is almost no control of language structure • (Virtually) nothing is correct. • Most of the errors are serious. • Very little is intelligible to a sympathetic native speaker.	• There is no evidence of detailed and complex language • The candidate copes only with "have" and "am". • There may be several examples of mother tongue interference. • Very few words are written correctly in the modern language. • English words are used. • There may be several examples of serious dictionary misuse.

HIGHER FOR CfE FRENCH
MODEL PAPER 1

Reading

Question		Expected Response
1.		• They are muslims
2.	(a)	• It was concerned with Christianity and Judaism • The focus is now on Islam
	(b)	• Islam has been rejected by public bodies • National government has closed its eyes • to the problems caused for Muslims by local politicians
3.	(a)	• Young people from Maghreb backgrounds have not been able to take their part in the construction of a new society
	(b)	• His parents and his heart are Algerian • For sport, he is French
4.	(a)	• The suburbs have lost their working class (popular) character • Immigrant families have settled there • Those of European background have left *Any 2 points from possible 3 for 2 marks*
	(b)	• In the areas where poor people live, there has taken root racism of the extreme right **and** radical Islam
5.	(a)	• The cultural gap/break between the Maghrebins and French society
	(b)	• Discuss the building of mosques • Provision of ground for cemeteries • Problems with distribution and control of halal meat *Any 2 points from possible 3 for 2 marks*
6.		• Recognise the role of the Republic in law • Confirm their belief in the values of the French legal system • Recognise clearly the equality of women and men *Any 2 points from possible 3 for 2 marks*
7.		Outline of possible response and evidence: The author does not think it is irretrievable: **Possible evidence includes:** • Author points out that it is a recent problem (the last 30 years) • Author says the government has often closed its eyes, implying it could do better • Author quotes Benzema as seeing himself as French • Author says modern politics are not reaching people, but then says what they need to do • Author gives a number of suggestions to improve things • Author finishes off by saying what Muslims need to do to improve things

Question	Expected Response
8.	Translation Les ruptures sociales sont maintenant très évidentes: **Social divisions (breakdowns, ruptures) are now very obvious:** les gens aisés avec leurs bons emplois **well-off people with their good jobs** réclament plus de liberté et d'indépendance, **demand more freedom and independence,** alors que les pauvres, ou sans emploi ou qui travaillent pour le SMIC* **while the poor, either (the) unemployed or (those) on minimum wages,** ont surtout besoin de sécurité et de solidarité. **need above all security and solidarity.**

Directed Writing

Please refer back to p 114 for advice on the general marking principles for Higher CfE French – Directed Writing.

Section 2 – Writing

Please refer back to p117–p119 for advice on general marking principles for Higher CfE French – Writing.

Section 1 – Listening

Item 1

Question		Expected Answer(s)
(a)		• Obtaining a certificate/diploma
(b)		• Start/find a job/profession/career
(c)		• It's part of their personal development/ growth • Or to learn new things and meet new people • To ask more of themselves *Any one of the above 3 points for 1 mark*
(d)	(i)	• The pressure is greater • You are seen as an adult and responsible for yourself *Any one of the above 2 points for 1 mark*
	(ii)	• You are not alone, everyone who leaves home experiences the same thing
(e)		• Studying part-time so you can work as well • Distance learning so you can stay at home
(f)		• He thinks it can be challenging but worthwhile if you are ready

Item 2

Question		Expected Answer(s)
(a)		• He wasn't qualified enough to get a good job
(b)		• In the world of IT (information technology)
(c)	(i)	• He wants to learn things
	(ii)	• The promotion of knowledge rather than the production of degrees
(d)		• Third year students are organised to tutor first year students
(e)		• First year students often find it hard to work in groups • Because they fail to see that sharing ideas is important (fundamental)
(f)		• In some courses/subjects only 25% of students pass their exam
(g)		• How to apply for courses • How to use a computer • How to take notes • Reading • How to do assignments and exams *Any 2 of the above 5 points for 2 marks*
(h)		• Perseverance **and** confidence (*both needed for the mark*)
(i)		• They said if he did not have good marks in maths at school, he would find it hard to get a maths degree • He was able to visit a university in his last year at school *Any one of above 2 points for 1 mark*

HIGHER FOR CfE FRENCH
MODEL PAPER 2

Reading

Question		Expected Response
1.	(a)	• Be 18 • Be of sound mind • Not be married already *Any 2 points from possible 3 for 2 marks*
	(b)	• Marriage was no longer available only to couples of different sex
	(c)	• Civil marriages normally take place at the town hall • Banns are published ten days before the wedding • Many people have a religious wedding after the civil wedding
2.		• Shopping **and** rent (*both needed for the mark*)
3.	(a)	• To allow gay couples to gain a status which included rights and obligations
	(b)	• Most people who have gone for a civil partnership are heterosexual • Only 4.5% of civil partnerships in 200 were of gay people • In 2010 the number of civil partnerships was almost as great as that of weddings
4.		• Its simplicity and its nontraditional (alternative) character • It is easier to form a civil partnership, and to finish one, than marriage and divorce are • Civil partnerships are 'lighter' and there are less responsibilities *Any 2 points from possible 3 for 2 marks*
5.	(a)	• You can now have a civil partnership in some town halls
	(b)	• When a woman is in a civil partnership she is still a 'Miss', and not a 'Mrs.' and does not have her partner's name
6.	(a)	• Adopt children together
	(b)	• To finish a civil partnership, one of the two partners only needs declare it over in court, without the other having to consent • For a marriage, you have to go through one of the divorce procedures

Question		Expected Response
7.		Outline of possible response and evidence: The author does not seem against civil partnerships. **Possible evidence includes:** • Author reports Janine's intentions without any negative comment • Author gives details of the growth in civil partnerships again without comment • Author explains it was originally intended for gay people, and again makes no negative comment on the changes • Author explains how they are easier, less traditional • Author quotes Valérie, who is a bit negative, but does not support her • Author explains how it is easier to end a civil partnership
8.		**Translation** La différence entre mariage et pacs devient de moins en moins avec le temps **The difference between marriage and civil partnership is growing less with time** mais il reste cependant bien des différences entre les deux institutions. **but there nevertheless remain many differences between the two.** Par exemple, dans un mariage l'époux comme l'épouse **For instance in a marriage both husband and wife** a le droit d'usage du nom de l'autre. **have the right to use the other's name.** Rien de tel pour les pacsés **It is not at all like that for civil partners.**

Directed Writing

Please refer back to p 114 for advice on the general marking principles for Higher CfE French — Directed Writing.

Section 1 — Listening

Item 1

Question		Expected Answer(s)
(a)		• The morning of the 14th of July (*all details needed for mark*)
(b)		• Federation Day **or** the end of the absolute monarchy
(c)		• Three years later **or** 1793
(d)	(i)	• There are balls (dances) • Fireworks • Parades or military processions *Any two of the above 3 points for 2 marks*
	(ii)	• In the overseas departments and/or territories • Places like Tahiti and Martinique *Any one of the above 2 points for 1 mark*

Question		Expected Answer(s)
(e)		• If France had qualified for the World Cup final
(f)		• He gives and explanation of where it comes from and what it is like now

Item 2

Question		Expected Answer(s)
(a)		• 24 hours a day, seven days a week
(b)	(i)	• 1.70€
	(ii)	• The first 45 minutes of every journey are free **or** you can do as many journeys as you want
(c)		• There are docking stations all over Paris
(d)	(i)	• It lets you hire a bike **or** it controls access to the bikes
	(ii)	• You can take a bike directly (without going through the "borne')
(e)		• It is a unisex/mixed bike • It has an adjustable saddle • It has a large basket • The lights stay on throughout the journey *Any two of the above 4 points for 2 marks*
(f)		• People between 14 and 26 in education/training
(g)		• Bank card • Cheque • Online subscription *Any one of the above 3 points for 1 mark*
(h)		• Authorisation from parent or guardian

Section 2 – Writing

Please refer back to p117–p119 for advice on general marking principles for Higher CfE French – Writing.

HIGHER FOR CfE FRENCH MODEL PAPER 3

Reading

Question		Expected Response
1.		• She had applied for a number of jobs • When she arrived at the interview she had forgotten which one it was
2.	(a)	• If you have friends who have had work experience/internships there • You could call them up and ask for information
	(b)	• To be more informed and able to react in the interview • To show your motivation and knowledge of the sector and the job/profession
	(c)	• If you apply again, you will have to be better informed **or** his interview was a catastrophe and he wasn't getting the job
3.	(a)	• Because the interviewer will probably have noted them and will concentrate on them
	(b)	• Periods of unemployment • A change in direction • A lack of satisfactory experience *Any 2 points from a possible 3 for 2 marks*
4.		• They will teach you to talk about yourself and to know how to sell yourself
5.	(a)	• Find out about where the interview is, public transport and parking or take account you could be caught in a traffic jam or your train might be late
	(b)	• About ten minutes early in case there are any forms to fill in
6.	(a)	• Wear clothes which fit the culture of the organisation you are going to • If you never will have to wear a suit at work, you don't have to wear one for the interview
	(b)	• The letter inviting you to the interview • Several copies of your CV in case you have to give them to people who don't have one • and the original, or a copy of, your certificates/diplomas *Any 2 points from a possible 3 for 2 marks*
	(c)	• Put them all in a folder so you don't seem disorganised

Question		Expected Response
7.		Outline of possible answers:
		The author gives the impression that a job interview is something you have to take very seriously; it is not straightforward.
		Possible evidence includes:
		• Writer starts off saying take half a day to prepare and start early
		• Writer gives the case of Alice who got it wrong
		• Writer says you absolutely must do research and gives details of what to do
		• Writer gives you another example of someone underprepared, Jean
		• Writer gives you details of all you should think about in your CV
		• Writer tells you to think about the dozen typical questions and have an answer for all of them
		• Writer goes into detail about how to avoid being late
		• Writer goes into detail about what to take with you and what to wear
8.		Translation
		Rafraîchissez-vous la mémoire avec des informations sur votre employeur actuel
		Refresh your memory with information about your current employer.
		On attend de vous que vous en sachiez
		They expect you to know
		beaucoup sur l'entreprise pour laquelle vous travaillez.
		a lot about the company that you work for.
		Préparez les questions que vous voulez vous-même poser.
		Prepare questions you yourself want to ask.
		N'oubliez pas qu'un entretien est aussi un échange.
		Don't forget an interview is also an exchange (of information).

Directed Writing

Please refer back to p 114 for advice on the general marking principles for Higher CfE French — Directed Writing.

Section 1 — Listening

Item 1

Question		Expected Answer(s)
(a)		• All the people and countries who speak French
(b)		• 220 million
(c)		• To support/develop the use of French • In the world/internationally and in diplomatic life

Question		Expected Answer(s)
(d)	(i)	• Defend cultural diversity on the Internet **or** make sure Francophones of all kinds participate
	(ii)	• Support the production of content in French • Put literary texts on line *Any one of the above 2 points for 1 mark*
(e)		• To launch a collaborative platform • Which provides resources in French
(f)		• He thinks French has to work hard to maintain its role in the world

Item 2

Question		Expected Answer(s)
(a)		• 220 000
(b)	(i)	• There are more than twice as many speakers of Breton than of Gaelic
	(ii)	• Gaelic is an official language in Scotland, Breton is a regional (minority) language
(c)		• It is seriously in danger
(d)	(i)	• It was in decline, but has grown stronger again
	(ii)	• There are (41) schools which now teach Breton • More books than ever are being published in Breton • Road signs are in both French and Breton *Any two of the above 3 points for 2 marks*
(e)		• There used to be less than 500 young (15-19) speakers of Breton • Now there are several thousand
(f)		• Several hours per week
(g)		• In the pronunciation

Section 2 — Writing

Please refer back to p117—p119 for advice on general marking principles for Higher CfE French — Writing.

Acknowledgements

Hodder Gibson would like to thank SQA for use of any past exam questions that may have been used in model papers, whether amended or in original form.